REMEMBER

"If any man will come after Me, let him first deny himself, and take up his cross and follow Me."

ST. MATTHEW, xvi, 24.

REMEMBER

Thoughts

on

*The End of Man,
The Four Last Things,
The Passion of Our Lord,
Human Suffering,
Humility and Patience*

COMPILED AND EDITED

BY

REV. F. X. LASANCE

Nihil Obstat
>   Arthur J. Scanlan, S.T.D.
>   *Censor Liborum*

Imprimatur
>   Patrick Cardinal Hayes
>   *Archbishop of New York*

New York, May 30, 1936

Copyright © 2020
All rights reserved.
ISBN-13: 9798626630619

FOREWORD

How shall I use this little book? A friendly voice replies: "Open it at sundown, in the morning, in the evening, at any leisure moment; read what you please and as much as you please, but read attentively, reflect seriously upon the thoughts suggested, make a firm resolution to aim persistently at perfection, and pray earnestly that you may become a saint."

* * *

This is the will of God, your sanctification.
—*1 Thess. iv, 3.*

* * *

I am the almighty God; walk before Me and be perfect.
Gen. xvii, 7.

* * *

Blessed is the man that shall continue in wisdom, and that shall meditate in his justice, and in his mind shall think of the all-seeing eye of God.
—*Ecclus. xiv. 22.*

* * *

Blessed is the man, whose will is in the law of the Lord; he shall meditate on His law day and night.

And he shall be like a tree, which is planted near the running waters, which shall bring forth its fruit in due season.

And his leaf shall not fall off, and all whatsoever he shall do, shall prosper.
—*Ps. i, 1,2,3.*

CONTENTS

FOREWORD v

PART I. THE END OF MAN

Remember.. 1
Remember, Man, That Thou Art Dust and Unto Dust Thou Shalt
    Return.. 2
Remember Thy Last End 7
Detachment 7
Happiness.. 8
A Happy Death 9
Deus Meus Et Omnia 10
God Craves Our Love 11
God Loves Me 12
All for the Glory of God 13
Asceticism 14

PART II. THE FOUR LAST THINGS

Remember the Last Things... 15
The Thought of the Last Things Is a Torch That Enlightens Us 16
The Value of Time 16
The Vanity of Earthly Possessions 17
The Folly of Sin 18
The Thought of the Last Things Is a Spur That Incites Us to Greater
    Effort.. 18
The Thought of the Last Things Is a Help That Supports Our
    Weakness 19
Personal Holiness 20

- Do Your Duty 21
- It Is Appointed Unto Men Once to Die (Heb. ix, 27) 22
- The Fear of Death 24
- Why Should We Stand in Such Fear of Death? 25
- The Heart of Mary Is Our Refuge 25
- The Cheerful Acceptance of Death 26
- Death Is a Law Established by God 26
- Death Is an Expiatory Sacrifice 27
- Death Is a Deliverance 28
- Death Is the End of Our Exile 28
- Resolution 29
- A Plenary Indulgence At the Hour of Death 29
- On the Particular Judgment After Death 30
- The Eternal Doom of Every Soul Is Decided by a Particular Judgment 31
- Hell 32
- The Pain of Loss 32
- Man Knoweth Not Whether He Be Worthy of Love or Hatred 33
- Purgatory 34
- Heaven 35
- The Essential Beatitude 36
- Other Joys of the Blessed Inhabitants of Heaven 37
- Everlasting Bliss 38
- Works of Mercy 39
- Eternity 41
- What Is This Life Compared With Eternity? 42
- Heavenly Glory Is Called a Crown 43
- Prayer for Perseverance 44
- Prayer to Overcome Evil Passions and to Become a Saint 44
- Prayer 45
- Requiescant in Pace 45
- The Efficacy of Prayer 46
- That Your Joy May Be Full 48
- Devotion to the Blessed Virgin Mary 49

My Mother, My Trust	49
Mary the Mother of Mercy and the Refuge Of Sinners	50
Devotion to St. Joseph	51
You Are Called to Be a Saint	53
The Fear of God	53
The Great Good God	54
Our Father, Who Art in Heaven	55
The Love of God	56
Effective Love	56
Affective Love	57
A Higher Kind of Love	58
As Much As I Can	59
The Love of Our Neighbor	60
Cultivate Cheerfulness	61
Fraternal Charity	62
Kindness	63
Success	63
Fidelity in Little Things	65
The Desire of Perfection	66
The Wings of Simplicity and Purity	68
The Ideal of Christian Perfection	69
The Loveliness of Jesus	69
The Habit Does Not Make the Monk	71
Blessed Are They That Suffer Persecution for Justice' Sake	72
Patience	73
Self-love	75
Mortification	76
The Devil, the World, and the Flesh	77
St. Francis De Sales On Mortification	78
But One Thing Is Necessary	79
The Mind of Christ	80
It Is Necessary That You Should Be Conformed to the Image and Likeness of Jesus Christ	84
The Sufferings of Christ	85

PART III. THE PASSION AND DEATH OF OUR LORD

The Way of the Cross 89
Via Crucis 90
Why Should I Suffer? What Have I Done? 91
The Love of Jesus Crucified 92
At Whose Hands Did He Suffer? 93
How Did He Suffer? 94
The Dream of the Holy Child 95
Our Lord Foretold His Passion to His Disciples 95
Hosannas 97
Lessons of Our Lord On the Eve of His Passion 98
Remember Me! 99
The Garden of Gethsemani 101
He Began to Grow Sorrowful 102
Fear, Sorrow, and Weariness..103
Our Saviour's Prayer 104
The Angel of Comfort 104
The Sleeping Disciples 105
It Might Have Been 106
The Traitor 107
Peter's Fall 109
I Know Not This Man 110
Peter's Repentance..111
Jesus Before Caiphas the High Priest..112
Jesus Is Condemned 113
Jesus Is Mocked and Blindfolded. He Is Left All Night in the Hands of
  His Guards...114
Christ Before Pilate...115
Hail, King of the Jews 116
Crucify Him 118
The Dreadful Torment At the Pillar..119
The Crowning With Thorns 122
The Meeting of Jesus and Mary...123
Simon of Cyrene Helps Jesus to Carry His Cross 124

Veronica Wipes Our Lord's Face 125
Jesus Nailed to the Cross 126
Mary At the Foot of the Cross 127
The Title of the Cross 129
Our Lord's Kingdom Is Not of This World 130
What I Have Written I Have Written 130
The First Word From the Cross 131
Forgive Them: for They Know Not What They Do 131
The Second Word From the Cross 133
The Third Word From the Cross 135
Salve Regina 136
The Fourth Word From the Cross 137
The Fifth Word From the Cross 139
The Sixth Word From the Cross 141
The Precious Blood 141
An Offering 143
Ejaculations 143
The Seventh Word From the Cross 143
Prayer 144
The Piercing of Christ's Side 145
Prayer Before a Crucifix 146
The Entombment 147
Mater Dolorosa 148
The Shadow of the Cross 150
The Vision of Calvary 150
The Risen Lord and His Mother 153
Regina Coeli 154
The Five Wounds of Christ 155

PART IV. HUMAN SUFFERING

Motives for Patience 157
Human Suffering 158
My Chalice Indeed You Shall Drink 159
The Royal Way: the Way of the Cross 161

Skull and Cross-bones At the Foot of the Crucifix 163
The Providence of God..165
Nothing Is Done Except in the Sight of God 165
Nothing Is Done Except by the Permission of God 166
Nothing Happens Except in Fulfillment of the Providential Plan of God 167
Conformity to the Will of God 168
Suffering Is a Superior Form of Action 169
Vicarious Suffering 170
A Sinner Is Slowly Breathing Out His Life 171

PART V. HUMILITY AND PATIENCE

Humility 173
Christ the Master of Humility...175
The Passion of Christ Is the Book of Humility.......................................177
One Unceasing Admonition in the Holy Scripture 178
Patience and Humility 179
Jesus Christ the Teacher and Model of Patience....................................182
Patience As the Perfecter of Our Daily Actions 183
"In Your Patience You Shall Possess Your Soul" 184
On the Cheerfulness of Patience 185
Through Many Tribulations We Must Enter Into the Kingdom of God 188
God Knows What Is Best for Us..189
Trust in God's Providence 190
The Thought of Hell a Motive of Patience 191
The Thought of Calvary a Motive of Patience 191
The Thought of Heaven a Motive of Patience...192
Mary and Martha..193
Little Faults and Little Virtues 195
The Life of Prayer...197
Humility and Patience 198
The Mother of Mercy..198
The Apostleship of Prayer..200

Morning Offering of the Apostleship of Prayer 202
The Five Wounds 202
The Apostleship of Prayer the Perpetuation of the Work of the
   Incarnation 204
In Sickness, Suffering and Sorrow 206
In Temptation and Humiliation 208
St. Francis Borgia, an Example of Humility and Self-contempt 210
St. Peter Damian 211
St. Paul of the Cross 212
St. Pius V 213
St. Alphonsus Liguori 215
St. Ignatius of Loyola 216
St. Columba 218
St. Francis Xavier 219
St. Peter Claver 221
St. Elizabeth of Hungary 222
St. Helen 224
St. John of the Cross 226
St. Andrew Avellino 227
St. Bruno 229
Remember 230
Prayer 234
The Eternal Years 234
Home, Sweet Home 236
Ave Maria 238

REMEMBER

PART I.
THE END OF MAN

Remember

Meditate on the admonition of the Wise Man: "In all thy works remember thy last end, and thou shalt never sin."
—*Ecclus. vii, 40.*

Reflect how true it is that the remembrance of the four last things has a marvelous efficacy to restrain the soul from sin, and to disentangle the heart from inordinate affections to the things of this world—to honor, wealth, and pleasure.

Hardened sinners have often been converted from their wicked ways to a penitential life by the terror of these thundering truths: *death, judgment, hell, eternity.* Meditation on these tremendous truths has sent numbers into deserts or religious houses, there to secure their eternal salvation by a saintly life; moreover, the considerations of such sublime truths have generally laid the first foundation even of the most eminent sanctity.

Oh, what lessons may we not learn among the silent monuments of the dead, who attracted attention and made some noise heretofore in the world, but now are thought of no more!

What salutary exhortations may we not daily receive by attending in spirit the trials at the great bar; by going down while we are alive into the darksome dungeons below, and viewing with dread the torments of the damned; and by ascending up into heaven, and contemplating those blessed mansions of eternal bliss prepared as a reward for the momentary labor and sufferings of the servants of God?

Let us daily frequent these schools to learn the science of the saints. Let us resolve to think often on these important subjects which concern so intimately our everlasting welfare; it will prepare us for a holy death; it will teach us to be always in readiness for judgment; it will keep us out of hell; it will bring us to heaven.

* * *

Remember my judgment: for thine also shall be so. Yesterday for me, and today for thee.

—*Ecclus. xxxviii, 23.*

REMEMBER, MAN, THAT THOU ART DUST AND UNTO DUST THOU SHALT RETURN

Alas! How prone we are to forget this truth! Our relatives, our friends, our acquaintances fall away from us—snatched by the hand of death—and we forget that we must follow them.

"Today for me," they say, "and tomorrow for you." Yet we live as though we could count on many tomorrows.

True; I may live to a good old age, but what is a good old age?

You answer: ninety years; and what will ninety years appear when the end comes at last and eternity lies before me! How like a dream, how brief, how fleeting! "All those things are passed away like a shadow, and like a post that runneth on, and as a ship, that passeth through the waves, whereof, when it is gone by, the trace cannot be found, nor the path of its keel in the waters" (Wis. v, 9). Our Saviour warns us to be ready like servants waiting for their master, with loins girt and lamps burning in our hands; for He will come as a thief in the night. "Watch ye, therefore, because you know not the day nor the hour" (Matt. xxv, 13).

It is appointed unto men once to die, and after this the judgment.

—Heb. ix, 27.

Man's days are as grass, as the flower of the field, so shall he flourish. For the spirit shall pass in him, and he shall not be: and he shall know his place no more.

—Ps. cii, 15, 16.

* * *

The mystery and the horror of death which prevailed in pagan times, and even among the Hebrews before the captivity, no longer exist. To a pagan, death was simple horror. It was the quenching of the cheerful flame of life; the loss of this sun, this earth, and all that can give enjoyment. There was a widespread feeling that it was not utter extinction; but if existence continued beyond the tomb, it was an existence unsubstantial and gloomy, as of ghosts and shadows.

To us who believe, death has many sides. There is much to fear; much to long for; much to labor for; much to trust to God for. Death has its joyful side and its mournful side. Doubtless with the most of us the mournful side predominates, and rightly so. It is not every one who can meet death with a *Te Deum*, like St. Aloysius and St. John Fisher. Considering our sins, the uncertainty of our repentance, the dangers of the last moments, the terrible interests at stake, we have much reason to fear. Death was meant as a punishment for the world's sin. And, therefore, even Christian faith, even the light of Christ's resurrection shining on the open tomb, cannot appease the shudderings, the repugnances, the physical torture of the act and the apprehension of death.

* * *

Let us then go forward, in thought, to the day of our death. It may, indeed, be much nearer than we think. This year, this month, tomorrow, this very night—we know now how soon it may be. For the day and the hour are fixed and certain. Suppose that it has come, and that we lie upon the bed whence we shall never rise. Probably our death will be sudden; sudden in its coming upon us, sudden in its consummation. Experience shows that most men do not expect Death, even when old age or infirmity might have let them understand that Our Lord was knocking at the door.

Let me, then, whilst now there is time, enter seriously into the thought of my wasted life. For has it not, up to this time, been in great part wasted? Have I not lived for foolishness, for that which passeth away, for that which cannot help me on my death-bed? Shall I not begin now at least—and begin from this very moment? O Jesus! give me Thy strength to begin a new life, a life of prayer, of serious watching over my passions, of total and complete surrender to my God!

Happy are the hands that are accustomed in life to be lifted up as we shall long to lift them up in the day of trouble, that lonely night of death; happy the hands that are not weighted with heavy fetters—that are pure and free, and know where to find their Heavenly Father.

* * *

Imagine that you are lying on your death-bed. Think of the inevitableness of that hour; of its pain, its abandonment, its fears, its temptations. Then accept it—and accept each of its circumstances; make a profound *act of conformity* of your will with that of your Heavenly Father, in regard to time, place, manner and surroundings. Make your own the words of Jesus: "Father, into Thy hands I commend my spirit!" They are the words of that thirtieth psalm which begins: "In Thee, O Lord, have I hoped, let me never be confounded." How many saints—as St. Nicholas, St. John of the Cross, and St. Catherine of Siena—have died with those words on their lips! What better preparation for death than perfect resignation!

Our Lord and Saviour wishes us to face the thought of judgment without undue terror or excitement. And therefore whilst He has revealed its terrors, He has not made it appear difficult to prepare for it. He has, as is usual with Him, pointed to one or two very common duties, and has promised that if we are faithful in these the judgment may be awaited with confidence.

* * *

"Judge not, and you shall not be judged." To judge others means to dwell uncharitably on the faults and weaknesses of our neighbor—or, what is worse, to reveal them and comment upon them. It is one of the commonest of sins. It is found among all ranks and degrees, wherever there is intercourse and conversation. It is found within the walls of convents almost as much—though not perhaps to such a serious degree—as in the drawing-room and the cottage. To strive to repress unkind conversation and unkind feeling is to be in earnest in loving God with our whole heart. Therefore, it is to secure for ourselves safety in the day of judgment.

* * *

"As you do to others, so also will my Heavenly Father do to you." This refers to kind actions. In order, therefore, to make sure of safety at the judgment, we cannot do better than study to show kindness to one another. If rich and well-to-do people are kind, they are safe; but the kindness must be true kindness. It must be a kindness that is anxious for the immortal souls which our heavenly Father chiefly longs for—which gives or procures instruction, sacraments, and good example. It must be a kindness which not only bestows money, but also comforting words; a kindness which not only gives what is superfluous to the giver, but is given at the cost of sacrifice and trouble.

—*Bishop Hedley.*

* * *

The sting of death is sin.

—*1 Cor. xv, 56.*

* * *

I must work the works of Him that sent me, whilst it is day; the night cometh, when no man can work.

—*John ix, 4.*

And in doing good, let us not fail. For in due time we shall reap, not failing.

—*Gal. vi, 9.*

I thought upon the days of old: and I had in my mind the eternal years.

—*Ps. ixxvi, 6.*

The numbers of the days of men at the most are a hundred years: as a drop of water of the sea are they esteemed; and as a pebble of the sand, so are a few years compared to eternity.

—*Ecclus. xviii, 8.*

Remember Thy Last End

Man has been created to praise God our Lord, to show Him reverence, and to serve Him, and by so doing to save his own soul; and everything else on the face of the earth has been created for the sake of man and to help him to attain the end for which he was created. Hence it follows that he must make use of these things insomuch as they help toward that end, and if ever they stand in his way, he must shake himself free from them.

—*St. Ignatius Loyola.*

* * *

What doth it profit a man, if he gain the whole world, and suffer the loss of his own soul? Or what exchange shall a man give for his soul?

—*Matt. xvi, 26.*

* * *

Therefore, whether you eat or drink, or whatsoever else you do, do all to the glory of God.

—*1 Cor. x, 31.*

Detachment

Detachment, as we know from spiritual books, is a rare and high spiritual virtue. . . . To be detached is to be loosened from every tie which binds the soul to the earth, to be dependent on nothing sublunary, to lean on nothing temporal; it is to care simply nothing what other men choose to think or say of us, or do to us; to go about our work, because it is our duty, as soldiers go to battle, without a care for the consequences; to account credit, honor, name, easy circumstances, comfort, human affections, just nothing at all, when any religious obligation involves the sacrifice of them. It is to be reckless of all these goods of life on such occasions.

—Cardinal Newman: Historical Sketches.

* * *

Jesus said to His disciples: If any man will come after Me, let him deny himself, and take up his cross, and follow Me. For he that will save his life, shall lose it; and he that shall lose his life for My sake, shall find it.

—Matt. xvi, 24, 25.

* * *

He that loveth father or mother more than Me, is not worthy of Me: and he that loveth son or daughter more than Me, is not worthy of Me.

—Ibid, x, 37.

* * *

Everyone that striveth for the mastery, refraineth himself from all things: and they, indeed, that they may receive a corruptible crown; but we an incorruptible one.

—1 Cor. ix, 25.

Happiness

The human heart craves and seeks unceasingly for happiness. Many find but a small measure of happiness in this world, because they lose sight of their eternal destiny—the object of their creation—which is to know God, to love Him, to serve Him, and to be happy with Him forever. "Thou shalt love the Lord thy God with thy whole heart; and thou shalt love thy neighbor as thyself."

(Matt. xxii, 33, 39.) The whole law depends on these two commandments; so Our Lord Himself assures us. The fullest measure of happiness even here on earth is attained by harmonizing one's conduct with the commandments of God, by doing well one's duties to God and man; for this means the possession of a peaceful conscience, a clean heart, a sinless soul; and this is essential to happiness.

* * *

Have pity on thy own soul, pleasing God, and contain thyself: gather up thy heart in His holiness: and drive away sadness far from thee.

—*Ecclus. xxx, 23, 24.*

A Happy Death

Whatever the ultimate number of years, all will see their last birthday and the last day of their lives. That day will be either of all the days they have lived the best and happiest, or of all the days that they have lived the miserable and fatal termination. A happy death is not the same as a painless death. The happiest death ever died was that whereby, under the torment of the cross, our Saviour overcame sin and death and hell. St. Lawrence died a happy death on the gridiron, and St. Thomas More by the headsman's axe. To die as softly as one drops off asleep, and awaking to find an angry Judge and an everlasting fire, is not a happy death. A happy death is death in the state of grace: that, and that alone, means eternal salvation. But though that is a happy death, there is yet a happier, and still a happiest. It is a happier death when one dies in the state of grace, owing little debt to God's justice in the shape of temporal punishment, whether for mortal sins forgiven in the past or for venial sins: for such a death means short purgatory and speedy paradise. Happiest death of all he dies, who dies in the state of grace, having done with substantial fidelity all the work and precisely the work of his life, the special work that God created him to do. This death is most like the death of Christ, who said on His dying day: "Father I have done to the end the work that Thou gavest Me to do: it is accomplished" (John xviii, 4; xix, 30).

—Rickaby: Ye Are Christ's.

DEUS MEUS ET OMNIA

My God and my All!

This was the favorite ejaculation of St. Francis of Assisi. Let us take it as our own.

With two wings a man is lifted up above earthly things: that is, with simplicity and purity.

Simplicity must be in the intention, purity in the affection.

Simplicity aims at God, purity takes hold of Him and tastes Him.

No good action will hinder thee if thou be free from inordinate affections.

If thou intend and seek nothing but the will of God and the profit of thy neighbor, thou shalt enjoy eternal liberty.

If thy heart were right, then every creature would be to thee a mirror of life and a book of holy doctrine.

There is no creature so little and contemptible as not to manifest the goodness of God.

—The Imitation of Christ.

* * *

With all thy strength love Him that made thee.

—Ecclus. vii, 32.

* * *

Let us love God, because God first hath loved us.
—*1 John iv, 19.*

Yea, I have loved thee with an everlasting love.
—*Jer. xxxi, 3.*

GOD CRAVES OUR LOVE

Let us look at the tray in which the Bible discloses Him to us in successive dispensations. He plants an Eden for His new-made creatures, and then comes to them Himself, and the evenings of the young world are consecrated by familiar colloquies between the creatures and their Creator. He tests their love by the lightest of precepts; and when they have broken it, clear above the accents of a strangely moderate anger are heard the merciful promises of a Saviour. Then come centuries of mysterious strife, like Jacob wrestling with God by the tinkling water of the midnight stream. No sin seems to weary Him. No waywardness is a match for the perseverance of His love. Merciful and miraculous interventions are never wanting. No gifts are thought too much or too good, if the creatures will but condescend to take them. On the Mesopotamian sheep-walks, in the Egyptian brick-fields, in the palm spotted wilderness, among the vineyards of Engaddi, by the headlong floods of harsh Babylon, it is always the same. God cannot do without us. He cannot afford to lose our love. He clings to us; He pleads with us; He punishes only to get love, and stays His hand in the midst; He melts our hearts with beautiful complainings; He mourns like a rejected lover or a suspected friend; He appeals to us with a sort of humility which has no parallel in human love.

—*Father Faber.*

* * *

Thou lovest all things that are, and hatest none of the things, which Thou hast made; for Thou didst not appoint or make anything, hating it. But Thou sparest all: because they are Thine, O Lord, Who lovest souls.

—*Wis. xi, 25-27.*

God Loves Me

God loves me—God desires my love. He has asked for it, He covets it, He prizes it more than I do myself! I would fain tell the poor trees, and the little birds that are roosting, and the patient beasts slumbering in the dewy grass, and the bright waters, and the wanton winds, and the clouds as they sail above me, and that white moon, and those flickering far-off stars, that God desires my love, mine, even mine! And it is true, infallibly true.

* * *

To love God because He desires our love, to love Him because He first loved us, to love Him because He loves us with such a surpassing love, to love our Creator because He redeemed us, and our Redeemer because He created us, to love Him as our Creator in all the orders of nature, grace, and glory, and finally to love Him for His own sake because of His infinite perfections, because He is what He is—this, and this alone, is religion.

* * *

Only serve Jesus out of love! Only serve Jesus out of love, and while your eyes are yet unclosed, before the whiteness of death is yet settled on your face, or those around you are sure that that last gentle breathing was indeed your last, what an unspeakable surprise will you have had at the judgment-seat of your dearest

Love, while the songs of heaven are breaking on your ears, and the glory of God is dawning on your eyes, to fade away no more forever!

—*Father Faber.*

* * *

Thou shalt love the Lord thy God with thy whole heart, and with thy whole soul, and with thy whole mind, and with thy whole strength.

—*Mark xii, 30.*

ALL FOR THE GLORY OF GOD

The love of God is not only to reside in our heart, but ought also to show itself in our conversation and to regulate all our words and actions, so as to give each one of them its due perfection. And this is loving God with our *whole strength*. This constant aiming at perfection in our daily and ordinary actions is one of the most important lessons of a spiritual life, and is the true practice of loving God with our whole strength. Now, this perfection of our ordinary actions, depends upon the purity and perfection of the intention from which these actions flow. The intention is pure when it aims at God alone; it is perfect when it does all for the love of God, and for the greater glory of God. "Whether you eat or drink, or whatsoever else you do, do all for the glory of God," says the Apostle (1 Cor. x, 31). The meanest action in life is ennobled by this intention; it becomes even an act of divine love, and a new step to unite the soul to God. So that the readiest way to come to love God with all our strength is to direct the whole of our actions to Him, by the pure and perfect intention of ever doing His holy will, and procuring in all things His greater glory.—*Challoner.*

Asceticism

In Holy Writ we are thus admonished; "Whatsoever thy hand is able to do, do it earnestly" (Eccles. ix, 10). "I have found that nothing is better than for a man to rejoice in his work" (Ib. iii, 22). "And I have known that there was no better thing than to rejoice and to do well in this life" (Ib. iii, 12). "*Age quod agis*" is therefore a good maxim in the spiritual life. "Do what you are doing," with your whole heart; do it well, do it perfectly. With a joyful heart do your duty at all times for the love of God. To do the will of God! To do that which God wills, and as He wills it, interiorly and exteriorly, and because He wills it! This is the asceticism which we should practise, namely, the asceticism which aims at the perfect discharge of every duty.

"When we will what God wills," says St. Alphonsus, "it is our own greatest good that we will; for God desires what is for our greatest advantage. Let your constant practice be to offer yourself to God, that He may do with you what He pleases." God cannot be deceived, and we may rest assured that what He determines will be best for us. Can there be a better prayer than this; "God's will be done!" "All that is bitter," says St. Ignatius Loyola, "as well as all that is sweet in this life, comes from the love of God for us."

My God, I believe most firmly that Thou watchest over all who hope in Thee, and that we can want for nothing when we rely upon Thee in all things; therefore I am resolved for the future to have no anxieties, and to cast all my cares upon Thee. "In peace in the selfsame I will sleep and I will rest; for Thou, O Lord, singularly hast settled me in hope." (Ps. iv, 9, 10).

PART II.
THE FOUR LAST THINGS

REMEMBER THE LAST THINGS

Let us adore the Holy Spirit inviting us to remember and frequently to meditate on the last things: *Death, Judgment, Heaven, and Hell*. In this thought, He tells us, we will find a powerful safeguard against sin. "*In all thy works remember thy last end, and thou shalt never sin*" (Ecclus. vii, 40).

Our Lord inculcates the same teaching many times in the Gospel, repeatedly placing before us the thought of the last things. At one time He gives us the picture of two roads, the broad highway that leads to perdition and the narrow path that leads to eternal life.

In another place He describes the folly of the rich man who, while surrounded with an abundance of earthly goods, destroyed his barns so as to build larger ones. He was delighted with the prospect of having henceforth nothing to do but enjoy the riches he had amassed. But God said to him: "Thou fool, this night do they require thy soul of thee: and whose shall those things be which thou hast provided?" (Luke xii, 20.) Was it not Jesus Christ Himself who enunciated this memorable maxim that has caused the conversion of so many saints: "What shall it profit a man, if he gain the whole world, and suffer the loss of his soul?" (Mark viii, 36.)

We have also the parable of the rich man cast into hell while the poor Lazarus rests in the bosom of Abraham and there enjoys the delights of heaven.

* * *

I must work the works of Him that sent Me, whilst it is day: the night cometh, when no man can work.

—*John ix, 4.*

* * *

The Thought of the Last Things Is a Torch That Enlightens Us

It recalls three fundamental truths that we should always keep before our eyes: the value of time, the vanity of earthly possessions, and the folly of sin.

The Value of Time

The Holy Ghost tells us that the life of man is like smoke that soon vanishes, a bit of light steam that rises up only to disappear immediately.

"What is your life? It is a vapor which appeareth for a little while, and afterwards shall vanish away" (James iv, 15).

But from the point of view of our last end, time presents an entirely different aspect. If employed according to the will of God, it is worth an eternity of happiness. "For that which is at present momentary and light of our tribulation, worketh for us . . . an eternal weight of glory" (2 Cor. iv, 17). So it is a precious possession that we ought to employ with great care, a treasure the waste or loss of which we ought keenly to regret.

The Vanity of Earthly Possessions

What are they, these goods that an eager world pursues as if they were its supreme happiness—what are they to the man who meditates on the last things, who always values the things of earth from eternity's point of view? They should be desired not merely for the sake of possession but to promote the glory of God and the good of souls. And when we consider their value in connection with death, judgment, heaven, and hell, we understand what is meant by the vanity of earthly possessions, we appreciate the evil consequences of inordinate attachment to them. Now the goods of eternity are of such a nature that we are sure of possessing them if only we make ourselves worthy to receive them. Heaven's reward is enduring and will render us for ever happy; whereas worldly possessions are uncertain, they can not bring us contentment and, in any event, must be given up at death.

* * *

Give alms out of thy substance, and turn not away thy face from any poor person: for so it shall come to pass that the face of the Lord shall not be turned from thee.

According to thy ability be merciful.

If thou have much give abundantly: if thou have little, take care even so to bestow willingly a little. . . .

Eat thy bread with the hungry and the needy, and with thy garments cover the naked.

—*Tob. iv, 7-9, 17.*

Cast thy bread upon the running waters: for after a long time thou shalt find it again.

—*Eccles. xv, 1.*

THE FOLLY OF SIN

What is sin in the light of our soul's eternal welfare?

It is an evil that reason disapproves; furthermore, it is an act which affords us but temporary indulgence or satisfaction of some passion, some fleeting pleasure, and renders us liable to eternal separation from God, unending punishment in hell. Rather than forego some sinful enjoyment or satisfaction we take such frightful chances with our immortal soul. "*Remember thy last end, and thou shalt never sin*" (Ecclus. vii, 40).

THE THOUGHT OF THE LAST THINGS IS A SPUR THAT INCITES US TO GREATER EFFORT

We should place ourselves in thought before those terrible events that will be the end of all our temporal interests; we should often say to ourselves: "This life through which I am hastening so recklessly will have an end; perhaps very soon will come the last of my days; then, when death violently separates me from all temporal affairs, I shall stand at God's judgment seat to account for every moment of my earthly sojourn, for my good and evil deeds, for my use and abuse of God's graces." My sentence at that dreadful moment will be either heaven or hell, an eternity of bliss or of torment. Supposing ourselves on the eve of this great event, would we not be less concerned about things of earth than about our heavenly interests? Would we not be more watchful to preserve our conscience pure from every sin; would we not exercise that constant vigilance which Jesus Christ so often recommends in the Holy Gospel? It is from eternity's point of view that our life will be judged and we would do well to estimate the value of our acts from this same standpoint. Life is given us that we may prepare for another world.

Let us live, then, as if in very fact our eternity were about to begin.

* * *

O that they would be wise and would understand, and would provide for their last end.

—*Deut. xxxi, 29.*

The Thought of the Last Things Is a Help That Supports Our Weakness

The Christian life to which we are called by divine grace requires great courage to resist the temptations that assault us from all sides.

But from what source shall we derive this energy and courage? We will place ourselves in the presence of approaching death, of the judgment that awaits us, of the happy or wretched eternity that must follow. We will say to ourselves: "To merit heaven and avoid hell can I not surmount this temptation, overcome these desires, or perform this act of virtue?" What is the sacrifice that will last but a time when compared with the enduring suffering of hell or the eternal joy of heaven.

If the recollection of the last things does not produce in us the same heroic courage that it wrought in the saints of God, if it leaves us feeble and unable to make any generous or sustained effort, what is the cause? Is it not our failure to apply this thought to ourselves? It enters our souls without penetrating deeply, it makes but a passing impression upon us.

In imitation of the saints, let us meditate on the last things. In the midst of the occupations of life, let us never lose sight of eternity. Then we too will be strong against temptation. No inducement will cause us to break our resolutions, no temptation will overcome us, no obstacle stop us.

I resolve:

1. To meditate often on the four last things;

2. To judge everything from the point of view of eternity;

3. At the beginning of every important work to propose to myself this question, which one of the saints was wont to ask himself: "What does this count for eternity?"

In all thy works remember thy last end, and thou shalt never sin.

* * *

With him that feareth the Lord, it shall go well in the latter end, and in the day of his death, he shall be blessed.

—*Ecclus. i, 13.*

Personal Holiness

"This is the will of God, your sanctification" (1 Thess. iv, 3).

"Be ye holy, because I the Lord your God am holy" (Lev. xix, 2).

Personal holiness is the goal that every individual must strive after. This is the one thing that is necessary. All other things are subsidiary and means to that end. No truth can be of more practical importance than this, the answer to the first question of the catechism. God placed me in this world that I may develop in me the image of His Son, that I may become holy as He is, that I may grow in perfection to the manner that my Father in heaven is perfect. "Be you therefore perfect as also your heavenly Father is perfect." We are troubled about many things, why not simplify our endeavors and seek the best part, the only part that comprises all the rest? That part is in plain language to do at every moment what is right, what is morally best.

* * *

Walk before Me and be perfect.

—*Gen. xvii, 1.*

DO YOUR DUTY

There are those who imagine that a life of holiness consists of days spent in prayer and mortification, that priests and nuns only can be holy, that one must achieve extraordinary things, be for instance a missionary in foreign lands, become a martyr at the stake, that saints do not eat and drink, barter and sell, work in factories, sit in a banker's chair, marry and give in marriage, as ordinary mortals do. There cannot, of course, be a more egregious mistake. Holiness consists in doing ordinary things extraordinarily well. No life was more ordinary than that of Our Lady at Nazareth, none more commonplace than that of St. Joseph at the carpenter's bench; could any have been more holy? To attend to the things that divine Providence ordains and because it is thus ordained, even though they amount to nothing but days of drudgery, that is holiness. We have met or have heard of so-called convent drudges, who would rise at four every morning, attend to cattle, see to the dairy, scarcely find time to assist at Mass, harrow and dig in the fields, all day be solicitous about the temporal needs of a young community, in the evening be overwhelmed with fatigue and hardly able to keep awake to "get in their prayers". They would lovingly complain that they could spend no time in the chapel at the Master's feet, and fear that they would have nothing precious to offer to God on the day of the general accounting. But they were doing their duty; they were keeping close to God; unknown to themselves they were leading holy lives and hoarding up treasures that rust and moth cannot consume. Let us repeat to ourselves, this is God's will, our sanctification, and this sanctification consists in doing every moment what is right, doing it thoroughly, cheerfully, steadily as Our Lord would do it, if He were in our place.

—*Fr. Brinkmeyer: Conferences of a Retreat.*

* * *

The days of David drew nigh that he should die, and he charged his son Solomon, saying:

I am going the way of all flesh: take thou courage, and show thyself a man.

—*3 Kings ii, 1, 2.*

It Is Appointed Unto Men Once to Die (Heb. ix, 27)

As every life on earth has had a beginning, so it must have an end. At some moment, determined from all eternity by the will of God, each life makes its appearance in the created world and takes its place in the company of creatures. Then, when its mission is accomplished, it disappears, vanishes. History is but a picture of succeeding existences that take the places of one another in perpetual changes.

On all creatures this law is imposed. The plant that grows in the soil, the animal endowed with more perfect life, is not exempted from it.

Nor is man. His life, too, begins, passes through the different stages, and is ended. His pilgrimage here on earth has a fixed limit which he is powerless to overstep.

God has given many things over to the domain of man. He has permitted him to delve into the secrets of nature, to discover its hidden laws, to bring nature into further subjection that it may serve his needs the better. But a moment will come when all his earthly power will vanish in death.

A moment will come, therefore, when I too must pass away, when my life, like a flame deprived of fuel, will be extinguished, when they will say of me what I have said of so many others: "*He is dead*", or "*She is dead.*" My body will turn into dust and my soul will undergo the terrible judgment of God's justice. This earth is not my final resting place. Here below is not my fixed and permanent abode. Earth is a place of probation.

Why, then, should I fix my heart on what must pass so quickly, why think so little of the inevitable end which every moment draws closer? So many things recall this end. The very land that I tread under foot is a vast graveyard. And is not the thought of death repeatedly and insistently forced on my attention? The diseases that assail me and the innumerable accidents that threaten me show clearly that, like the rest of men, I too am condemned to die. No thought ought to be more familiar than this one of death. However, by a strange blindness I scarcely ever turn my attention to it. Innumerable interests, the acquisition of knowledge, business, the care of my health, all occupy my attention. But death, watching perhaps at my very door, ready to seize its prey, inevitable death, that will usher in the great day of eternity, hardly costs me a thought.

The life of most men is passed in this dangerous forgetfulness. To see them, to hear them, to follow them in their daily occupations, you would suppose they were convinced that the present life would have no end, that the earth would be their eternal abode.

O Lord, dispel such a deplorable illusion. Since this life of mine must end, since, sooner or later, death will mark its close, turn my eyes away from present attractions and impress the thought of death deep down in my soul so that, when the moment comes for me to pass from this life, I may be neither surprised nor terrified.

I resolve therefore:

To use every opportunity to recall the thought of death, and, like the Psalmist, to keep in mind the eternal years.

* * *

The end of all is at hand. Be prudent, therefore, and watch in prayers.

—*1 Peter iv, 7.*

* * *

Be you then also ready: for at what hour you think not, the Son of Man will come.

—*Luke xii, 40.*

The Fear of Death

Why should we stand in such fear of death?

Our sins, it is true, ought to alarm us; but the thought of the merits of Christ ought to reassure us. Our sins are great in themselves and in their number; but they are finite, while the virtue of the merits of Jesus Christ is infinite. Our evils are great, but the blood of Our Saviour is a powerful remedy for all evils. I owe, it is true, ten thousand talents to the justice of God; but as great as this debt is, I am not insolvent, since I hold in my hands the price of the blood of Jesus Christ which is of infinite value. I dare say that I pay God more than I owe Him, when I offer Him the precious blood of His divine Son. I know that God will grant me pardon for my crimes when I ask it through the merits of Christ. Since He has given me His Son, can He refuse me anything?

Why Should We Stand in Such Fear of Death?

I should fear indeed the judgment of God; but His mercy ought to reassure me. Is God less merciful than He is just? If His justice terrifies me, His mercy ought to calm my fears. I fear His justice, but I should hope in His mercy, since He Himself teaches me that His "mercy exalteth itself above judgment" (James ii, 13). God draws from His own heart the motives of His mercy; He draws from our hearts the motives of His justice. During life we experience the reign of God's mercy, and after death the reign of His justice. If we have recourse to His mercy during life, if we have not a presumptuous confidence in it, we shall have no cause to fear His justice after death. If my salvation depended on the dearest friend that I have in the world, I would rest in peace. Yet what greater friend have I than Jesus Christ who has loved me so much that He has given His life for me?

The Heart of Mary Is Our Refuge

Why should we stand in such fear of death? We have, it is true, terrible enemies arraigned against us; we must repel the assaults of demons whose delight it is to make us companions in their misery. But however violent their rage may be, however redoubtable their efforts, we have, in the Blessed Virgin, a most powerful resource; we have in her heart a refuge where we will be secure from all the wiles of Satan. If Mary is our help, we should no longer fear the power of hell; her name causes the demons to tremble. Can we doubt that she is willing to aid us since she is our mother, and the kindest of all mothers? I am a wretched sinner, it is true, but Mary is the refuge of sinners and the mother of mercy.

When you are troubled by an immoderate fear of death, think of the mercy of God, the merits of Jesus Christ and the tenderness of our blessed Mother.

"Ecce Deus salvator meus: fiducialiter agam et non timebo" (Is. xii, 2). "Behold God is my Saviour; I will deal confidently and will not fear."

—*Nepveau: Meditations.*

The Cheerful Acceptance of Death

Let us adore the Son of God humbly submitting to the general law of death.

From the beginning of His life He offered himself, a victim to appease the divine justice. Many times during the course of His mortal life did He testify His desire to accomplish this great sacrifice. And finally in the Garden of Olives, on the night before His immolation, again He accepted the bitter chalice that His heavenly Father presented to Him. "Not My will," He said, "but Thine be done."

By His own striking example, our divine Master teaches us with what humble submission we ought to accept the decree of death to which we are all condemned. If we can not say with St. Paul that we have a "desire to be dissolved and to be with Christ," we should at least accept God's decree in humble submission.

Death Is a Law Established by God

It is a Decree of God's providence, of His wisdom and goodness, of His supreme will which rules the universe. God has also determined the time, the place, and the manner of our death, thus asserting His sovereign dominion over life.

If we truly love God, we will readily accept His decrees, whether such obedience entails comfort or hardship, life or death.

My God, I thank Thee for having given me life. Thou hast willed that after a few years this life shall end. For this I thank Thee also. "For so hath it seemed good in Thy sight" (Matt. xi, 26).

Death Is an Expiatory Sacrifice

Sin is the unjust preference of the creature to the Creator. It was through sin that death came into the world and with death came the countless trials and difficulties by the patient endurance of which we are chastened and rendered acceptable to God. Death is the greatest expiation we can offer since it takes from us our riches and pleasures and even the most precious of our earthly possessions, life itself.

Death is, therefore, par excellence, the expiatory sacrifice which God requires of us sinners. When we consider it from this point of view and gladly submit to it, we are performing a holy and most meritorious act. If we accept death with these dispositions, it is divested of much of its hideous repulsiveness, and assumes a noble character. We see not only the weakness and the nothingness of the creature but also the self-sacrifice of a victim. The death-bed becomes an altar; the expiring body a host; the disease, a consuming fire; the soul freely offering itself in expiation for sin, the priest.

* * *

O death, where is thy victory? O death, where is thy sting? Now the sting of death is sin.

—1 Cor. xv, 55, 56.

* * *

Precious in the sight of the Lord is the death of His saints.

—Ps. cxv, 75.

Death Is a Deliverance

It is a deliverance which we should accept hopefully and lovingly. It is a relief from sorrow and suffering. It is a release from sin. The desire to avoid sin inspired the saints with their intense zeal for eternal life, made them long for death. "I am at the end of my course," said one of God's elect just before the soul returned to its Creator, "I will sin no more." When we too understand what a great misfortune it is to offend God, then death will appear desirable to us.

* * *

Who can understand sins? From my secret ones cleanse me, O Lord.

—Ps. xviii, 13.

* * *

They that commit sin and iniquity are enemies to their own soul.

—Job xii, 10.

Death Is the End of Our Exile

Our home is not here on earth. As the great Apostle once said: "We have not here a lasting city, but we seek one that is to come."

Heaven is our home where we shall spend eternity with Christ. "We know," says the inspired word, "that if our earthly house of this habitation be dissolved, that we have a building of God, a house not made with hands, eternal in heaven." So death should be joyfully accepted by us as the end of sorrow, of sin, and of exile. "Woe is me, that my sojourning is prolonged! . . . My soul hath been long a sojourner" (Ps. cxix, 5).

Resolution

The fear of death is good and salutary. It is a powerful incentive to preserve me from sin and to strengthen my fervor and zeal. But I should adopt a nobler, more meritorious, more Christian attitude towards death. Since Thou, my God, hast decreed it, I should accept it generously and lovingly.

My Lord and My God, I am ready to die at whatever time and place Thy providence has determined, in whatever manner thou hast chosen for me, whether it shall be expected or unexpected, now or after a longer pilgrimage. I accept death without complaint or murmur. Life, the most precious gift in my possession, I offer to Thee, happy thus to acknowledge Thy absolute power and my absolute dependence.

I resolve to accept my death in humble submission to Thy holy will.

"To die is gain" (Philip. i, 21).

A Plenary Indulgence At the Hour of Death

By a decree of the Sacred Congregation of Indulgences of March 9, 1904, Pope Pius X granted a plenary indulgence at the moment of death to all the faithful who, on any day they may choose, shall receive the sacraments of Penance and Holy

Eucharist and make the following act with sincere love toward God.

O Lord my God, I now at this moment readily and willingly accept at Thy hand whatever kind of death it may please Thee to send me, with all its pains, penalties, and sorrows.

* * *

On the Particular Judgment After Death

Since death is so certain and the time and manner of it so uncertain, it would be no small comfort if a man could die more than once; that so, if he should have the misfortune once to die ill, he might repair the fault, by taking more care the second time. But, alas! we can die but once; and when once we have set our foot within the gates of eternity, there is no coming back. If we die once well, it will be always well; but if once ill, it will be ill for all eternity! O dreadful moment! upon which depends an endless eternity.

Set your house in order now; and for the future, fly from sin, the only evil that makes death terrible. Live always in those dispositions in which you would gladly be found at the hour of your death.

* * *

"Watch ye therefore, (for you know not when the lord of the house cometh: at even, or at midnight, or at the cock-crowing, or in the morning,)

"Lest coming on a sudden, he find you sleeping.

"And what I say to you, I say to all: Watch."

—*Mark xiii, 35, 36, 37.*

The Eternal Doom of Every Soul Is Decided by a Particular Judgment

Consider that the soul is no sooner parted from the body but she is immediately presented before the Judge, in order to give an account of her whole life, of all that she has thought, said, or done during the abode in the body; and to receive sentence accordingly. That the eternal doom of every soul is decided by a particular judgment immediately after death, is what we learn from the Gospel, in the example of Dives and Lazarus. And the sentence that is passed here will be ratified in the General Judgment at the last day. Christians, how stand your accounts with God? What would you be able to say for yourselves, if this night you should be cited to the bar? It may, perhaps, be your case. Remember that your Lord will come when you least expect Him. Take care, then, to be always ready.

Consider that in order to prevent the judgment of God from falling heavy upon us after death, we must take care now during our life to judge and chastise ourselves, by doing serious penance for our sins. Thus, and only thus, shall we disarm the justice of God, enkindled by our sins. Let us follow the advice of Him who is to be our Judge, who calls upon us all to watch and pray at all times; that so we may be found worthy to escape these dreadful dangers, and stand with confidence before the Son of man. Ah! let this judgment be always before our eyes. Let us daily meditate on the account that we are one day to give. Let us never forget that there is an eye above, that sees all things; that there is a hand that writeth down all our thoughts, words, and deeds in a great account-book; that all our actions pass from our hands to the hands of God; and that what is done in time passeth not away in time, but shall subsist after all time is past. "Oh, that they would be wise, and would understand, and would provide for their last end!" (Deut. xxxii, 29.)

—*Challoner: Think Well On't.*

Hell

Consider that as it is said in Holy Writ, that, "The eye hath not seen, nor ear heard, neither hath it entered into the heart of man, what things God hath prepared for them that love Him" (1 Cor. ii, 9), so we may say truly; with regard to hell's torments, that no mortal tongue can express them, nor heart conceive them. Beatitude, according to divines, is a perfect and never-ending state, comprising at once all that's good, without any mixture of evil. If, then, damnation be the opposite to beatitude, it must needs be an everlasting deluge of all that is evil, without the least mixture of good, without the least glimpse of comfort; a total deprivation of all happiness, and a chaos of all misery.

The Pain of Loss

Consider in particular, that pain of loss, which, in the judgment of divines is the greatest of all the torments of hell.

As long as sinners are in this mortal life they in many ways partake of the goodness of God, "who maketh His sun to rise upon the good and bad: and raineth upon the just and the unjust" (Matt. v, 45). All that is agreeable in this world, and all that is delightful in creatures, all that is comfortable in life, is all in some measure a participation of the divine goodness; no wonder, then, that the sinner, while he in so many ways partakes of the goodness of God, should not in this life be sensible of what it is to be totally and eternally deprived of Him. But in hell, alas! those unhappy wretches shall find that in losing their God they have also lost all kind of good or comfort which any of His creatures heretofore afforded; instead of which, they find all things now conspiring against them, and no way left of diverting thought from this loss, which is always present to their minds, and torturing them with inexpressible torments.

Man Knoweth Not Whether He Be Worthy of Love or Hatred

I have deserved hell as often as I have committed mortal sin, yet God has delivered me from this greatest of evils as often as I have repented. What gratitude then do I not owe God for having preserved me from so great a misfortune? If God could call one of the lost souls from hell and deliver it from its punishments, what an obligation would rest upon that soul! But does not this same obligation rest upon me, since God has so often delivered me from hell? How many there are who have been hurled into hell after one mortal sin? What mercy has He not shown to me! I know that I have not merited this mercy, and that I owe it entirely to God's bounty. How inexcusable then am I, if I am ungrateful for it.

I know not whether I be worthy of love or hatred. Even the greatest saints feared, and what should be my sentiments? Should not this uncertainty cause me fear and excite me to penance?

If it were necessary to cut myself off from the world, and to pass the remainder of my life in performing the most severe penances, so that I might be secure from the fear of hell, should I hesitate for a moment to do so? But that is not demanded. God asks me only to restrain a passion or to give up some pleasure. If I do not do as God commands me, how does my conduct accord with my faith?

When some cross or humiliation is laid upon you, say to yourself: What is this in comparison with the pains of hell which I have so often deserved?

* * *

There are just men and wise men, and their works are in the hand of God: and yet man knoweth not whether he be worthy of love or hatred.

—*Eccles. ix, i.*

Purgatory

If we could realize all the pains of purgatory, we would better understand the severity of divine justice, the wickedness of venial sin, and the worth of penitence.

The severity of divine justice. For, those whom God chastises in purgatory, keeping them in a dismal exile and afflicting them with dreadful pains, are His friends, His children, the heirs of His kingdom! In truth, if I look deeper into the thing, I should not wonder that He, with unrelenting anger, punishes and scourges the damned souls in hell, since these are His enemies, who hate and blaspheme Him; but I should fear and tremble at His justice, seeing how He chastens with untold afflictions the souls in purgatory, who love Him and are loved by Him with a fatherly love. Such holy fear shall be to me like a protecting shield against all temptations: O Lord, *pierce Thou my flesh with thy fear, for I am afraid of Thy judgments* (Ps. 118).

The wickedness of venial sin. For, it is for such sins that He, the upright Judge, so severely punishes those beloved souls! And perhaps, till now, I regarded as trivial many faults, and rashly made myself guilty, saying: it is but a venial sin! And all the while, I was gathering wood, hay and straw, fuel for the fire which would burn me, the wood of avarice, the hay of sensuality and the straw of pride and vainglory. Henceforth I will be wiser and, as far as possible for human frailty, I will dread and shun venial sin.

The worth of penitence. In this life, there is mercy; in the next, I can expect nothing but justice. . . . *Now* God is easily moved to pity through the trials and crosses which we patiently bear or willingly take up; when we have paid off one thousandth part of our debt, He readily forgives the whole; but *then*, like an exacting creditor, He will claim the last farthing and rightly too! For, if now we spurn His kindness and refuse the easy means of shortening our debt, later we shall have no reason to grumble at His justice.

Therefore, I will gladly do penance for my sins and patiently bear the ills and pains of this life; for whatever we may suffer here is short and little; it helps us on toward perfection and increases our future harvest of merits. But, in purgatory, pains are worse and they last longer; nor are they of any avail to increase our share of heavenly glory. . . . I will also be diligent, whilst I live, in gaining indulgences. Lastly, I will devote myself to works of mercy, either material or spiritual; I will be zealous to help the poor suffering souls, and thus make unto myself friends who may receive me into the everlasting dwellings (Luke xvi, 9).

—*Lescoubier, Monthly Recollection.*

* * *

It is a holy and wholesome thought to pray for the dead that they may be loosed from sins.

—*2 Mach. xii, 6.*

Heaven

Consider that if God's justice be so terrible in regard to His enemies, how much more will His mercy, His goodness, and His bounty declare themselves in favor of His friends. Mercy and goodness are His favorite attributes, in which He most delights. "His mercies," says the Royal Prophet, "are above all His works" (Ps. cxliv). What then must this blessed kingdom be, which in His goodness He has prepared for His beloved children for the manifestation of His riches, His glory, and magnificence for all eternity? A kingdom which the Son of God Himself hath purchased for us at no less a price than that of His own most precious blood. No wonder then that the Apostle cries out, "That eye hath not seen, nor ear heard, neither hath it entered into the heart of man, what things God hath prepared for them that love Him" (1 Cor. ii, 9). No wonder that this beatitude is defined by divines "a perfect and everlasting state, replenished by all that is good, without the least mixture of evil."

A general and universal good, filling, brimful, the vast capacity of our affections and desires, and eternally securing us from all fear or danger of want or change. Ah! here it is in the servants of God, that the Psalmist's words are fulfilled: "They shall be inebriated with the plenty of Thy house: and Thou shalt make them drink of the torrent of Thy pleasure" (Ps. xxxv, 9); even of that fountain of life which is with Him, and flows from Him into their happy souls forever and ever.

THE ESSENTIAL BEATITUDE

Consider that although this blessed kingdom abounds with all that can be imagined good and delightful, yet there is one sovereign Good, in the sight, love, and enjoyment of which consists the essential beatitude of the soul, and that is God Himself, whom the blessed ever see face to face, and by the contemplation of this infinite beauty are set on fire with a seraphic flame of love, and, by a most pure and amiable union, are transformed in a manner into God Himself; as when brass or iron in the furnace is perfectly penetrated by the fire, it loseth its own nature, and becometh flame and fire. Ah, happy creatures! what can be wanting to complete your joys, who are in perfect possession of your God, the overflowing source of all good, who have within and without you the vast ocean of endless felicity? Oh, the excessive bounty of Our God, who giveth to His servants, in reward of their loyalty, so great a good, which is nothing less than Himself, the immense joy of angels! Oh! shall not that suffice, my soul, to make thee happy which makes God Himself happy?

Other Joys of the Blessed Inhabitants of Heaven

Consider the blessed inhabitants of His heavenly kingdom, those millions of millions of angels of whom the prophet Daniel, having seen God almighty in a vision, tells us that "Thousands of thousands ministered to Him: and ten thousand times a hundred thousand stood before Him" (Dan. vii, 10); that infinite multitude of saints and martyrs and other servants of God, of both sexes, gathered out of all nations, tribes, and tongues; and above them all the Blessed Virgin Mother of God, Queen of saints and angels; their number is innumerable.

They are all most noble, most glorious, most wise, most holy. They are all of blood royal, all kings and queens, all children and heirs of the Most High God; ever beautiful and ever young; crowned with wreaths of immortal glory, and shining much brighter than the sun. Their love and charity for one another are more than can be conceived. They have all but one heart, one will, one soul; so the joy and satisfaction of every one are multiplied to as many fold as there are blessed souls and angels in heaven, by the inexpressible delight that each one takes in the happiness of all, and every one of all the rest. Christians, let us imitate their virtues here, that we may come to their happy society hereafter, and with them sing to our God the immortal songs of Sion.

Everlasting Bliss

Consider that what renders all the joys of heaven and the felicity of the blessed completely great is the eternity of their bliss, and the infallible certainty and security which they enjoy that their happiness is ever linked with God's eternity; that as long as God shall be God they shall be with Him in His blessed kingdom. O my soul! how pleasant, how delightful it is to look forward in this vast eternity, and there to lose thyself in this happy prospect of endless ages! Oh! bless thy God, who has prepared these immortal joys for the reward of such small services, and designed them from all eternity for thee! Nor shall this immense eternity render these enjoyments any wise disagreeable or tedious by the length of the possession; but, as God is an endless ocean of all good, and His divine essence an inexhaustible, infinite treasure of delights, so the happiness of those that eternally enjoy Him shall be always fresh, always new. Conclude, then, Christian soul, to contemn and forsake all that is earthly and temporal, and from this hour to begin a journey toward the glorious heavenly and eternal kingdom. There thou shalt find all that thy heart can desire immortal honors, immense riches, pure and eternal pleasures, life, health, beauty never fading. Oh! this alone is thy true home, the land of the living.

—*Challoner, Think Well On't.*

* * *

Meditate often and seriously on the happiness of heaven. Such meditations, besides deepening our knowledge of God, and of the things He has prepared for those who love Him, have a wonderful power of detaching our hearts from the transitory pleasures and honors of this world. They, moreover, create in our soul an unquenchable thirst for the vision and possession of God, while they infuse into us a new courage to battle manfully against all the obstacles which beset our path in the practice of virtue.

Expect the Lord, do manfully, and let thy heart take courage, and wait thou for the Lord.
—*Ps. xxvi, 14.*

* * *

He that shall persevere to the end he shall be saved.
—*Matt. xxiv, 13.*

* * *

I have fought a good fight, I have finished my course, I have kept the faith.

As to the rest, there is laid up for me a crown of justice, which the Lord, the just Judge, will render to me in that day: and not only to me, but to them also that love His coming.
—*2 Tim. iv, 7, 8.*

WORKS OF MERCY

At the end of the world, "the Son of Man shall come in the glory of His Father with His angels: and then will He render to every man according to his works" (Matt. xvi, 27).

Then shall the books be opened, the book of God's law and the book of man's conscience. We may hide our sins now as much as we like; we may even hide them in the confessional; but then every eye shall see them. How shall I be able to endure that? Even the sins of the just will be laid bare; but the penance they have done for them and their other good works will so flood them with light that they will bring no shame to them, nothing but joy and thankfulness.

"Then shall the King say to them that shall be on His right hand: Come, ye blessed of My Father, possess you the kingdom prepared for you from the foundation of the world" (Matt. xxv. 34). Who would not wish to hear these words said to him? Will they not make up for a long life of self-restraint and self-conquest? "For I was hungry and you gave Me to eat; I was thirsty and you gave Me to drink; I was a stranger and you took Me in; I was sick and you visited Me; I was in prison and you came to Me." Then shall the just answer Him, saying; Lord, when did we see Thee hungry? . . . And the King, answering, shall say to them: "Amen, I say to you, as long as you did it to one of the least of these My brethren, you did it to Me." And if this is the reward of the corporal works of mercy, what of the spiritual works? What of converting the sinner, instructing the ignorant and the rest? "They that instruct many to justice, shall shine as stars for all eternity" (Dan. xii, 3).

"Then He shall say to them also that shall be on His left hand; Depart from Me, ye cursed, into everlasting fire, which was prepared for the devil and his angels. . . . And these shall go into everlasting punishment, but the just into life everlasting."

We must all be manifested before the judgment seat of Christ, that every one may receive the proper things of the body, according as he hath done, whether it be good or evil.

—2 Cor. v, 10.

And they that have done good things shall come forth unto the resurrection of life; but they that have done evil, unto the resurrection of judgment.

—John v, 28, 29.

Religion clean and undefiled before God and the Father, is this: to visit the fatherless and widows in their tribulation: and to keep one's self unspotted from this world.

—*James i, 27.*

For judgment without mercy to him that hath not done mercy. And mercy exalteth itself above judgment.

—*James ii, 13.*

ETERNITY

"I am not born for time," St. Stanislaus would say, "but for eternity." And indeed, we have not a permanent dwelling on earth, we are created for heaven. True, the godless say "reasoning with themselves, but not right . . . we are born of nothing, and after this we shall be as if we had not been . . . our body shall be ashes and our spirit shall be poured abroad as soft air. . . . Come therefore and let us enjoy the good things that are present and let us speedily use the creatures as in youth. . . . These things they thought, and were deceived; for their own malice blinded them" (Wis. ii, 1, 2, 3, 6, 21). But Our Lord has answered most clearly and emphatically: "These shall go into everlasting punishment; but the just into life-everlasting" (Matt. xxv, 46).

Whosoever then has received life shall live forever, whether in bliss or in woe; and after millions and millions of years and centuries, beyond any number we can conceive, there shall be no end of life; it shall still be a beginning of joy or sorrow. . . . When I depart from this world, there awaits me a blissful or a woeful eternity. . . . If I die in the love of God, my soul shall go to heavenly glory, see the face of God and enjoy in Him unspeakable joys, in the blessed company of angels and the communion of saints; and of such joys there shall be no end; they last forever. If

I die in mortal sin, without the love of God, hell is my dwelling-place; I suffer privation of the divine presence and awful torments in the Unquenchable fire; nor of these shall there be any end!

How foolish then to be so anxious about present trifles and never or seldom to think of eternity! How wise, on the contrary, to show by one's life that one is born, not for time, but for eternity; to think, to speak, to work for eternity; to have in mind future life and often to say with St. Aloysius: "What is this with regard to eternity?"

WHAT IS THIS LIFE COMPARED WITH ETERNITY?

What is this with regard to eternity?—What is this life compared with eternity? If you think of its duration, it must be thought to be nothing: "The number of the days of man at the most are a hundred years; as a drop of water of the sea so are they esteemed; and as a pebble of the sand, so are a few years compared to eternity" (Ecclus. xviii, 8).

If we look at eternity, what are *temporal goods*? Very easily they are made a snare of the devil, and for him who seeks or enjoys them unwisely, they prepare a wretched eternity. Therefore Christ says: "Amen, I say to you, that a rich man shall hardly enter into the kingdom of heaven" (Matt. xix, 23); and: "Woe to you that are rich; for you have your consolation" (Luke vi, 24). "For they, that will become rich, fall into temptation, and into the snare of the devil, and into many unprofitable and hurtful desires, which drown men into destruction and perdition" (1 Tim. vi, 9).

If we look at eternity, what are *honors and dignities of the world?*— Of themselves they give nothing, and "it is vanity to seek an honorable station or a high office" (Imit. i, 1). Moreover, they easily bring with them pride and sin; therefore it is written: "A most severe judgment shall be for them that bear rule . . . the mighty shall be mightily tormented" (Wis. vi, 6, 7).—"All honor which we receive from the world pleases the devil," says St. Hilary; because it puts us into the danger of losing humility and running to our perdition.

If we look at eternity, what are the *joys and pleasures* of this world? Let the Lord answer: "Woe to you that now laugh; for you shall mourn and weep" (Luke vi, 25). "It is a vanity to satisfy the desires of the flesh, and to seek what we shall have to rue later" (Imit. i, 1). It is an exchange of everlasting pain for the pleasure of a moment!

And lastly, what are the *troubles* of this life, if we look at eternity? St. Paul shall tell us: "I reckon that the sufferings of this time are not worthy to be compared with the glory to come" (Rom. viii, 18). "For that which is at present momentary and light of our tribulation, worketh for us above measure exceedingly an eternal weight of glory" (2 Cor. iv, 17). It is an exchange of everlasting bliss for the suffering of a moment!

Think on it and keep it in your mind! "In all thy works, remember thy last end, and thou shalt never sin" (Ecclus. vii, 40).
—*Lescoubier, Monthly Recollection.*

HEAVENLY GLORY IS CALLED A CROWN

Labor unceasingly for that "inheritance incorruptible and undefiled, and that can not fade, reserved in heaven for you" (1 Peter i, 4).—"Be thou faithful until death, and I will give thee the crown of life" (Apoc. ii, 10).

We must remember that heaven is a reward promised to them that deserve it through their good works. "Labor as a good soldier of Christ Jesus" (2 Tim. ii, 3); and if perchance the burden weighs heavy and the labor is hard, encourage yourself by looking up to the reward. Fulfil faithfully all your duties: "Be ye steadfast and unmovable, always abounding in the work of the Lord, knowing that your labor is not vain in the Lord" (1 Cor. xv, 58).

Heavenly glory is called a *crown*. Now, "he that striveth for the mastery is not crowned except he strive lawfully" (2 Tim. ii, 5). Fight then the good fight of the faith, the battles of the Lord; be steadfast and courageous; and soon "you shall receive a never-fading crown of glory" (1 Peter v, 4).

Heaven is the *kingdom* of God; we are its heirs. But it is the will and the law of God that "through many tribulations we must enter into that kingdom" (Acts xiv, 21), as Christ also had to "suffer and so to enter into His glory" (Luke xxiv, 26). So that the way to heaven is the way of the cross. Let us then, beloved of Christ, follow our beloved Master on the way of His passion, and "that which is at present momentary and light of our tribulation shall work for us above measure exceedingly an eternal weight of glory" (2 Cor. iv, 17).

Prayer for Perseverance

O Lord Almighty, Who permittest evil to draw good therefrom, hear our humble prayers, and grant that we remain faithful to Thee unto death. Grant us also, through the intercession of most holy Mary, the strength ever to conform ourselves to Thy most holy will.

* * *

Prayer to Overcome Evil Passions and to Become a Saint

Dear Jesus, in the Sacrament of the Altar, be forever thanked and praised. Love, worthy of all celestial and terrestrial love! Who, out of infinite love for me, ungrateful sinner, didst assume our human nature, didst shed Thy most precious blood in the cruel scourging, and didst expire on a shameful cross for our eternal welfare! Now, illumined with lively faith, with the outpouring of my whole soul and the fervor of my heart, I humbly beseech Thee, through the infinite merits of Thy painful sufferings, give me strength and courage to destroy every evil passion which sways my heart, to bless Thee in my greatest afflictions, to glorify Thee by the exact fulfilment of my duties, supremely to hate all sin, and thus to become a saint.

Prayer

O God, who hast prepared for those who love Thee good things which eye hath not seen, pour into our hearts the fervor of Thy love, that, loving Thee in all things and above all things, we may attain Thy promises, which surpass all desire.
—*Roman Missal.*

Non nobis, Domine, non nobis; sed Nomini Tuo da gloriam. Not to us, O Lord, not to us; but to Thy Name give glory.
—*Ps. cxiii, i.*

Requiescant in Pace

We have so close an acquaintance in this life with sorrow in all its forms, that we can well realize what it means to be suddenly set free from it forever. We know how intense is the feeling of relief when some violent nervous pain is removed, how after a long spell of toothache is over we lie down to sleep like a child tired out with play.

Now, if heaven meant nothing more than eternal rest; that is, lasting and conscious deliverance from all the ills of this weary pilgrimage, would it not even then be worth all that we are called on to pay down for it? But it means so much more than this; and if even on this earth the good can for a little space so flood our soul with joy, if an enchanting scene or a strain of exquisite music can so melt our hearts as to make us forgetful of all life's troubles, how will it be, think you, when the Lord of heaven and earth, the Source of all love and all beauty, lays Himself out to make His creatures happy? May we not be sure that He knows how to do it? Oh, in very truth: "Eye hath not seen, nor ear heard, nor hath it entered into the heart of man what things God hath prepared for them that love Him."

O God, grant that we may so pass through the good things of this life as not to lose those which are eternal.

* * *

I heard a voice from heaven, saying to me: Write: Blessed are the dead who die in the Lord. From henceforth now, saith the Spirit, that they may rest from their labors; for their works follow them.

—Apoc. xiv, 13.

And God shall wipe away all tears from their eyes: and death shall be no more, nor mourning, nor crying, nor sorrow shall be any more, for the former things are passed away.

—Apoc. xxi, 4.

There the wicked cease from tumult, and there the wearied in strength are at rest.

—Job iii, 7.

THE EFFICACY OF PRAYER

The Holy Scriptures are full of examples of the efficacy of prayer as a means of obtaining whatever we need to secure our salvation. It was by his prayer that the publican was justified, by her prayer that the Samaritan woman was converted; it was by his prayer that David obtained the forgiveness of his sin, and that the good thief on the cross was converted and received the promise of paradise. We find in Holy Writ also many examples of prayer as an efficacious means of obtaining even temporal favors. It was by prayer that Moses obtained the victory over the Amalekites; Elias obtained rain after a three years' drought; Manassas, his deliverance from prison and his restoration to his kingdom; Ezechias, the prolongation of his life; Solomon, wisdom; Susanna the proof of her innocence; Daniel, his deliverance from the lions; the blind man, his sight; and the Church, St. Peter's deliverance from prison and death.

"He who prays," says St. Alphonsus, "is certainly saved; he who prays not is certainly lost. All the blessed (except infants) have been saved by prayer. All the damned have been lost by not praying; had they prayed, they would not have been lost. And this is and will be their greatest torment in hell, to think how easily they might have been saved, had they only prayed to God for His grace; but the time of prayer is now over for them." St. Augustine is, then, right in calling prayer "the key of heaven."

—*Fr. Girardey, C.SS.R.; Popular Instructions on Prayer.*

The Lord is nigh to all them that call upon Him in truth; He will do the will of them that fear Him; He will hear their prayer, and will save them.

—*Ps. cxliv, 18, 19.*

That Your Joy May Be Full

Our Lord said to His disciples: "Amen, Amen, I say to you, if you ask the Father anything in My name, He will give it you. Ask, and you shall receive, that your joy may be full" (John xvi, 23).

Great indeed and very comforting are the promises made to prayer. *"Ask, and you shall receive."* It would seem from this that one has only to ask in the name of Christ and he is sure of getting what he wants; yet, common sense tells us that can not be the meaning intended. If it were, we Christians should ask for all the good things of life and get them, the hard and bitter things being left to those who had no faith; for, when any affliction threatened us, we should at once pray it away. It is evident, surely, that prayer is not meant to be simply an escape from suffering. Mark, now, that little clause: *"that your joy may be full"*; for therein lies the explanation of Our Saviour's words. What joy is He thinking of? Eternal joy, of course. He binds Himself, therefore, to give us whatever will help us on our road to heaven. He will indeed hear and answer all our prayers; but if we make foolish petitions, He will answer them in His own wise and fatherly way by giving us something better. If we let our children have everything they cried for we should soon see them in their graves; and if God were to grant us everything we ask of Him, we should never rise to a better life.

* * *

Love God all thy life, and call upon Him for thy salvation.
—*Ecclus. xiii, 18.*

* * *

Devotion to the Blessed Virgin Mary

Jesus and Mary are so closely united, that they can not well be separated. We can not love and honor the Son without loving and honoring the Mother. All the merit and glory of the Mother come from the Son, and all the honor that we render to the Mother is, at the same time, rendered to the Son. The heart is not divided by the devotion we have for Mary. On the contrary, it is united more strongly to the heart of Jesus. The confidence that we have in the protection of the Blessed Virgin does not diminish the confidence we should have in her Son. On the contrary, it increases it and renders it more just and efficacious. The love of Jesus for Mary is unbounded; therefore Mary's power is unbounded; and her love for me is in proportion to my confidence in her. How unbounded then should be my confidence! Loving and generous as she is, can she refuse to love one who loves and serves her? Since Jesus loves Mary with an infinite love, can He refuse to love those that she loves? Will He permit any one to be lost whom she desires to save? Will He suffer a heart that burns with love for His Mother to burn in the flames of hell?

My Mother, My Trust

How culpable would I be, if I should ever despair of the mercy of God, when I have for my mother the Mother of mercy. I will oppose the justice of the Son with the mercy of the Mother. Must not the one yield before the other? Will not the prayers of Mary be more potent to appease the justice of her Son, than my crimes are to excite it? I know that my salvation is assured when I leave it in the hands of Mary. If she does not obtain it, it will be the fault either of her power over her Son, or of her love for me: can I doubt of either without outraging both the Son and the Mother?

Can she be lacking in power over her Son, she to whom her Son has delegated in an especial manner His omnipotence; she who can do all things with her Son, and who has great intercession with her Son? The power of Mary ought to be measured by her dignity as Mother of God, by the love of her Son for her, by the grandeur of her obligations to Him, and by the title of Mediatrix of men with which He honors her.

Mary the Mother of Mercy and the Refuge Of Sinners

But if power is not wanting to Mary, neither is love for us wanting. "Nec facultas illi deest, nec voluntas" (St. Bernard). By becoming the Mother of God she became the mother of men. Christ, in giving His Mother to St. John, gave her likewise to all the faithful. We are then her adopted children; wretched children we are, it is true, but our miseries augment her love and her tenderness, because she is the Mother of mercy and the Refuge of sinners. Mary is the Mother of God, she is my mother. She has great intercession with her Son and her love for me is unbounded. Therefore, if I serve her well, if I place my confidence in her, should I not feel assured of my salvation?

Take the resolution to have a great devotion to the Blessed Virgin and a great confidence in her protection; but strive to merit her protection by being zealous in her service and faithful to her Son.

"Qui me invenerit inveniet vitam, et hauriet salutem a Domino" (Prov. viii, 35). He that shall find Me shall find life, and shall have salvation from the Lord.

"Totum nos habere voluit per Mariam, qui et ipsum filium nos habere voluit per Mariam" (St. Bernard). God who has given us

His Son through Mary, has willed that we should obtain the graces He has merited for us, by the intercession of Mary.

—*Nepveau: Meditations.*

* * *

Hail, full of grace, the Lord is with thee: Blessed art thou among women.

—*Luke i, 28.*

Devotion to St. Joseph

In what esteem ought we not to hold St. Joseph, who is called in Holy Scripture *a just man,* a man chosen by God to be the guardian of the Infancy of His Word Made Flesh, and the protector of the Blessed Virgin Mary!

St. Joseph lived with Him Who is the source of all graces and with her who is, as it were, the channel for distributing them, how many spiritual riches did he not receive from them!

Love of God, love of our neighbor, humility, patience, gentleness, kindness—all virtues shone in him and were carried to sublime heights. If thou desirest to give thyself up to the exercises of a devout and interior life, have recourse, in order to obtain the grace of them, to the intercession of a saint who practised them in so perfect a manner. The Church has erected to God temples in his honor; she has instituted feasts in his honor; she invites her children, by means of devotions which she has authorized, to look upon him as one of the most powerful protectors they have in heaven.

The name of Joseph is, in fact, specially invoked by all the faithful; they frequently unite it with the names of the sacred persons to whom he was so closely united—Jesus and Mary. If, at the time when Jesus and Mary lived at Nazareth, we had wished to obtain a grace, what more powerful mediator among men could we have employed than St. Joseph? Will he now have less credit with them? "Go, then, to Joseph" (Gen. xli, 55), that he may intercede for you. Whatever may be the grace you desire, God will grant his request.

But, above all, go to Joseph to obtain the grace of a good death. The common opinion that he died in the arms of Jesus and Mary has given cause for the great confidence which the faithful have, that, through his intercession they will enjoy as happy and as consoling an end. It may, in fact, be remarked that it is particularly at the hour of death that we reap the fruits of the devotion we had during life to this great Saint.

* * *

The Lord loveth the just.
—Ps. cxlv, 8.

* * *

The blessing of the Lord is upon the head of the just.
—Prov. x, 6.

* * *

Jesus, Mary, Joseph, I give you my heart and my soul.
Jesus, Mary, Joseph, assist me in my last agony.
Jesus, Mary, Joseph, may I breathe forth my soul in peace with you.

* * *

YOU ARE CALLED TO BE A SAINT

How often do we read in the Sacred Scriptures that we ought to be saints. Again and again has God declared His will in this regard.

"Be ye holy, because I the Lord your God am holy," was what He perpetually inculcated in the Old Testament; and in the New, the Son of God calls upon us all, Matt. v, 48: "Be ye perfect as your heavenly Father is perfect." All Christians are "called to be saints," Rom. 1, 7; "to be holy and without blemish in the sight of God in charity," Eph. 1, 4.

All are not commanded to work miracles, nor to exercise extraordinary austerities; nor to retire into deserts, to spend the whole time there in prayer; nor to sell all they have, and give it to the poor (for there have been many very great saints that have done none of these things): yet all are commanded to love God with their whole heart, and with their whole soul, and with their whole mind, and with their whole strength. Now this it is that makes saints, and this is of strict obligation to all. Do this, my soul, keep this commandment, and thou also shalt be a saint, but without this, none of those other things, nor all of them together, can make any one a saint.

* * *

Health of the soul in holiness of justice is better than all gold and silver.

—*Ecclus. xxx, 75.*

THE FEAR OF GOD

"Blessed is the man that feareth the Lord" (Ps. cxi, 1). Fear, in so far as it is one of the gifts of the Holy Spirit, has nothing in common either with the fear which seizes us in the presence of danger, or with the apprehension of sin which torments the scrupulous soul, or even with the Christian fear of the torments of hell. The fear of which we speak is a gentle fear, inspired by love and reverence for the eyes of God which are fixed upon us. For the sole reason that we love God, we are afraid that something may displease Him, either in our acts or our words, the thoughts of our mind or the slightest movements of our heart, upon which we know that His eyes are constantly intent; and this fear renders us circumspect in the whole of our conduct, careful in doing all things well, attentive to give to every one of our actions all the perfection of which it is capable. "A wise man," says Solomon, "feareth and declineth from evil; the fool leapeth over and is confident" (Prov. xiv, 16).

* * *

Behold the fear of the Lord—that is wisdom: and to depart from evil, is understanding.

—*Job xxviii, 28.*

* * *

The Great Good God

No one is more solicitous for our well-being for time and eternity than the great, good God. To make us understand this truth, He compares Himself to a shepherd seeking the lost lamb in the desert, and again to a mother, who can never forget her child: "Can a woman forget her infant, so as not to have pity on the son of her womb? and if she should forget, yet will not I forget thee" (Is. xlix, 15). Again, He compares Himself to a hen which shelters her young under her wings: "Jerusalem, Jerusalem, thou that killest the prophets, and stonest them that are sent unto thee, how often would I have gathered together thy children as the hen doth gather her chickens under her wings, and thou wouldst not!" (Matt. xxiii, 37). God encompasses us, as David says, in order to turn away from us every danger on the part of our enemies: "O Lord, Thou hast crowned us as with a shield of Thy good will" (Ps. v, 13). Ah! why do we not abandon ourselves entirely to the guidance of so good a father? Happy are they who allow themselves to be led by Almighty God as He wills and where He wills!

* * *

He will overshadow thee with His shoulders, and under His wings thou shalt trust.

—*Ps. xc, 7.*

OUR FATHER, WHO ART IN HEAVEN

Thou art my Father, O my God, and the Father of all, the rock of our salvation. Thou art my protector and my refuge; in Thee will I place my trust. If Thou be with me, who can be against me? I will cast my care upon Thee; for as a Father Thou dost love me and provide for my welfare. "We know that to them that love God all things work together unto good," says the Apostle (Rom. viii, 28). And Jesus Himself tells us to place our hope in Thee: "Behold the birds of the air; for neither do they sow, nor do they reap, nor gather into barns; and your heavenly Father feedeth them. Are not you of much more value than they? Be not solicitous for tomorrow. Seek ye first the kingdom of God, and His justice, and all these things shall be added unto you."

Jesus Himself directs us to address Thee as "Our Father," and to pray to Thee in His name with the utmost confidence: "Ask and it shall be given you, for every one that asketh, receiveth; if you being evil know how to give good gifts to your children, how much more will your Father who is in heaven give good things to them that ask Him" (Matt. vii, 7, 11).

Do thou, then, listen to my prayer. From the summit of heaven, where Thou dost dwell and where Thou art the supreme happiness of the blessed, look down upon me with loving-kindness and guard me as Thy child in all my ways. Keep me in Thy love and grant me perseverance in Thy grace, that I may one day see Thee face to face in my true fatherland, and bless and glorify Thee forever in the company of the saints.

* * *

I have loved thee with an everlasting love.
—*Jer. xxxi, 7.*

THE LOVE OF GOD

The love of God and of our fellow-men for God's sake, is, as we all know, "*the great commandment of the law.*" The highest sanctity can not reach beyond the perfect realization of the ideal expressed in this precept: "Thou shalt love the Lord thy God with thy whole heart and with thy whole soul and with thy whole mind. This is the greatest and the first commandment. And the second is like to this: Thou shalt love thy neighbor as thyself" (Matt. xxii, 37-39).

EFFECTIVE LOVE

"If you love Me," said Our Lord to His disciples, "keep My commandments."

This, which we may call "effective love," is the foundation of all. Religion does not consist, principally and fundamentally, in worth, and feelings, and outward observances (though these have their place, and are necessary as helps), but in the interior obedience of the heart, in the resolute submission of the will to God's law. "Not every one that saith to Me: Lord, Lord, shall enter into the kingdom of heaven; but he that doeth the will of My Father Who is in heaven, he shall enter into the kingdom of heaven." In the Garden of Olives Jesus said: "My soul is sorrowful even unto death." "He fell upon His face, praying, and saying: My Father, if it be possible, let this chalice pass from Me. Nevertheless not as I will, but as Thou wilt." . . .

"Again the second time, He prayed, saying: My Father, if this chalice may not pass away, but I must drink it, Thy will be done" (Matt. xxvi, 39, 42).

AFFECTIVE LOVE

God wishes to be loved not only with the *effective love* of the *will* but also with the *affective love* of the *heart*.

Indeed, we may say with confidence that this desire of God for our heart's love was one of the reasons why the eternal Word not only became man, but chose to live such a life and to die such a death as we know Him to have lived and died. He knew how difficult it is for us to form an idea of God, as God, and of His attributes. He would be born of a human mother; and who does not know how much of tender devotion and piety among Christians is due to this blessed choice. He would take a human Heart to love us with. Not content with telling us that the lot of the poor and the mourner is blessed, He would enroll Himself formally in the ranks of the poor, and would be Himself a Man of sorrows. He would be born in a wayside stable, that all might have easy access to Him. He would lie as an infant in His crib, that children might learn to love Him. And then, after all the moving events and incidents of His life here on earth, He would die hanging aloft upon the cross, that He might draw all hearts to Himself. Truly, in the words of Bishop Hedley, "Jesus Christ makes worship easy"; and one of the ways in which He makes worship easy is by providing great abundance of fuel wherewith to kindle the flame of *affective love*.

—*Lucas: In the Morning of Life (adapted).*

* * *

You know the grace of Our Lord Jesus Christ, that being rich, He became poor, for your sakes; that through His poverty you might be rich.

—*2 Cor. viii, 9.*

In this we have known the charity of God, because He hath laid down His life for us: and we ought to lay down our lives for the brethren.

—*1 John iii, 16.*

A Higher Kind of Love

From the Crib to the Cross Jesus was engaged in doing a great work: a work which is still going forward in the world. Now, friendship or love, if it rises beyond the level of mediocrity, is not content with avoiding offence to the person loved, or with affectionate and tender feelings. It leads us to interest ourselves in the undertakings of our friends, and this in such practical sort as to desire, if it be possible, to share in those undertakings, and to help with all our power in carrying them through. Our Lord does invite men to share in His great work, and He has made it possible for us to help Him in carrying it through. The test of love, of the higher grades of love, is readiness to cooperate in His great work for the salvation of mankind. Are we ready? Are we willing? This is a point which many persons do not consider half seriously enough.

As Much As I Can

It would be a very great mistake to suppose that this higher kind of the love of God which manifests itself in a desire to imitate Our Lord as closely as possible, and to share His work, is to be found only among priests and Religious, or that it is not attainable in its degree by every one of us. Many circumstances may concur to make it clear that any particular person is not called to the priesthood, or to the religious state. He may have the duty of supporting, or helping to support, his parents or other members of his family; he may be physically unfit, or unsuited by natural disposition, for the duties of a priest. But no disability, financial, physical, intellectual, or moral, can hinder him from loving Our Lord with all his heart. No obstacle can prevent him from taking, as his rule of conduct, not the law of parsimony, the principle of the man who asks: "How little can I do—what is the least that I must do—in order to save my soul?" but the law of generosity, the principle of the man whose question is always: "Is there anything more that I can do to please Our Lord better, and to follow Him more closely than I have hitherto done?" There is plenty of work for God and the Church to be done by laymen; and the law of generosity is aptly expressed by the Stonyhurst motto: *Quant je puis*: "As much as I can." Whether we be priests or whether we be laymen, in generosity toward God, at whatsoever apparent or momentary cost to ourselves, lies the secret of true joy and peace. *Quant je puis*; not "as little as I am obliged," but "as much as I can."

* * *

Let us make sacrifices; let us pray and suffer, in union with Jesus, for the conversion of sinners, for the welfare of the Church, and for the Propagation of the Faith.

With Christ I am nailed to the cross.
—*Gal. ii, 19.*

* * *

"I Paul am made a minister: who now rejoice in my sufferings for you and fill up those things that are wanting of the sufferings of Christ, in my flesh, for His body, which is the Church."
—*Col. i, 24.*

THE LOVE OF OUR NEIGHBOR

Consider by what rules we are to be directed and regulated in the exercise of the love of our neighbor. The old commandment of the divine law was to love every neighbor as ourselves.

The new commandment of the Gospel of Christ is to love every neighbor *"even as Christ has loved us."* Have we ever seriously reflected upon the perfection of the love which these rules require of us?—"To love our neighbors as ourselves." Oh, how tender is the love we bear ourselves! how intent upon our own welfare! how sensible of everything that we apprehend as an evil to us! Is the love of our neighbors anything like this? Do we treat them as we would desire to be treated ourselves? Are we concerned at the evils which befall them, as if they had befallen ourselves? I fear we cannot say it. Again, "To love our neighbors as Christ has loved us." Oh, what a love is this! He has laid down His very life for the love of us; and this without any desert on our side: we were His enemies by sin. Can our love for our neighbors stand the test of this rule? Are we willing to part with so much as our own humor, our convenience or inclination, our pleasure or satisfaction, for the love of our neighbors, and rather than give them occasion of grief or sin? If not, how far are we from loving our neighbors as Christ has loved us!

—*Challoner.*

* * *

Every one shall help his neighbor, and shall say to his brother: Be of good courage.

—*Is. xli, 6.*

Cultivate Cheerfulness

One of the most important qualities to be cultivated in domestic life is cheerfulness. As sunshine brings out the flowers and ripens the fruit, so does cheerfulness develop in us all the seeds of good—all that is best in us. Cheerfulness is a duty we owe to others. There are some people whose smile, the sound of whose voice, whose very presence, seems like a ray of sunshine bringing happiness to others.

We must all have our trials, and times will come when we feel "out of tune" with life, but others likewise have their crosses to bear, and why should we add to their weight by causing them to share ours? Constant cheerfulness can only be acquired by constant unselfishness, and arises from determination to make ourselves, as St. Paul tells us, "all things to all men."

* * *

Rich or poor, if his heart is good, his countenance shall be cheerful at all times.

—*Ecclus. xxvi, 4.*

Fraternal Charity

What is fraternal charity? It is love for our neighbor practised in *thought, word* and *deed.*

This love is the distinctive mark of the elect: "By this shall all men know that you are My disciples, if you have love one for another" (John xiii, 35).

Our Lord tells how to practise charity: "All things therefore whatsoever you would that men should do to you, do you also to them" (Matt. vii, 12).

Kind thoughts, gentle words, and putting in practice the corporal and spiritual works of mercy is the fulfilling of the law.

If each one would love his neighbor the world would become a paradise—the rich would help the poor, capitalists would pay just wages to laborers, the strong would assist the weak, enemies would be forgiven; it could be said of the whole world as it was of the early Christians, they have "but one heart and one soul" (Acts iv, 32).

St. Paul teaches us the excellence of this virtue in these words: "For he that loveth his neighbor, hath fulfilled the law" (Rom. xiii, 8).

No better epitaph can be placed on a man's tomb than "He loved his neighbor."

—*Fr. John M. Macklin, C.P.: Brief Explanation of Religious Questions.*

* * *

This commandment we have from God, that he who loveth God, love also his brother.

—*7 John iv, 21.*

KINDNESS

If we reflect upon it, kindness is but the outcome and exemplar of the divine precept: *Thou shalt love thy neighbor as thyself.* There is nothing we personally so much appreciate as kindness. We like others to think of us kindly, to speak to us kindly, and to render us kindly actions and in a kindly manner. Now, we should know how to put ourselves in the place of others, and thus we should testify to them that kindness that we value so much ourselves.

* * *

I shall pass through this world but once; if there is any good that I can do, any kindness that I can show to any human heart, for the love of Jesus, let me do it now; let me not defer nor neglect it; for I shall not pass this way again.

* * *

Whosoever shall give to drink to one of these little ones a cup of cold water only, in the name of a disciple, amen I say to you, he shall not lose his reward.

—*Matt. x, 42.*

SUCCESS

"One thing I do; forgetting the things that are behind and stretching forth myself to those that are before, I press toward the mark" (Philipp. iii, 13, 14).

1. Every one desires to succeed in life. A man who desired ultimate failure would justly be regarded as a lunatic. If I am to carry out my desire, I must look round me and see what sort of men succeed.

2. When I look at successful men, I find in all three characteristics:

(1) A spirit of cheerfulness and confidence. They know how to look at everything from its best side. Hence I must pray for confidence.

(2) A spirit of perseverance. They are not discouraged by failures. They recover themselves without delay. What a lesson for me not to lose heart, but to say: When I fall I will rise again, and that promptly!

(3) A spirit of single-mindedness. They keep the end in view steadily before them. If I am to attain to the end of my life, to succeed in coming to God at last, I must keep Him always before me.

3. What can make my life so happy as this, to know that I am drawing nearer to God? Yet there will be dark times and days of despondency. Still down at the bottom, beneath the surface, there will be hope and peace, even amid the darkness.

Pray for cheerfulness and an earnest purpose to live for God.

—*R. F. Clarke, S.J.*

* * *

In Holy Writ we are thus admonished: "Whatsoever thy hand is able to do, do it earnestly" (Eccles. ix, 10). "I have found that nothing is better than for a man to rejoice in his work" (Ib. iii, 22). "And I have known that there was no better thing than to rejoice and to do well in this life" (Ib. iii. 12). *"Age quod agis"* is therefore a good maxim in the spiritual life. "Do what you are doing," with your whole heart; do it well, do it perfectly. With a joyful heart do your duty at all times for the love of God. To do the will of God! To do that *which* God wills, and as He wills it, interiorly and exteriorly, and *because* He wills it! This is the asceticism which we should practise, namely, the asceticism which aims at the perfect discharge of every duty.

Let us also bear in mind the axiom: *"Sat cito si sat bene"*: "One does that fast enough which is well done." And let us often during the day raise our heart to God by short and fervent aspirations and the renewal of a pure intention, e.g.: For God alone! My God and my All!

* * *

Behold, short years pass by, and I am walking in a path by which I shall not return.

—*Job xvi, 23.*

* * *

I spoke with my tongue: O Lord, make me know my end.

And what is the number of my days: that I may know what is wanting to me.

—*Ps. xxxviii, 5-6.*

* * *

In doing good, let us not fail. For in due time, we shall reap, not failing.

Therefore, whilst we have time, let us work good to all men, but especially to those who are of the household of the faith.

—*Gal. vi, 9, 10.*

FIDELITY IN LITTLE THINGS

The best perfection is the performance of common things in a perfect manner. A constant fidelity in little things is a great and heroic virtue.

—*St. Bonaventure.*

* * *

Our fidelity to little things, commonplace duties, is a truer index of love than the acceptation of greater difficulties. It requires great strength of character and solid virtue to do little things well. There is no human applause to be won, nothing to arouse enthusiasm, no subconsciousness that we are doing something praiseworthy. To be gentle and patient at home, to keep one's temper month after month amid the friction and petty annoyances which we encounter in our daily life, needs more courage than it requires to perform some heroic act at which the world marvels. All have not the opportunity of doing great things, but all can be faithful in little things, and so merit to hear from the lips of our dear Lord the *"Well done, good and faithful servant; enter thou into the joy of thy Lord."*

—*Madame Cecilia: Cor Cordium.*

* * *

He that is faithful in that which is least is faithful also in that which is greater.

—*Luke xvi, 10.*

THE DESIRE OF PERFECTION

As it is impossible to arrive at perfection in any art or science without ardent desires of its attainment, so no one has ever yet become a saint, but by strong and fervent aspirations after sanctity. "God," observes St. Teresa, "ordinarily confers His signal favors on those only who thirst after His love." "Blessed," says the Royal Prophet, "is the man whose help is from Thee: in his heart he hath disposed to ascend by steps in the vale of tears. . . . They shall go from virtue to virtue" (Ps. lxxxiii, 6, 7, 8). "The path of the just," says Solomon, "as a shining light goeth forward and increaseth even to perfect day. The way of the wicked is darksome: they know not when they fall" (Prov. iv, i 8, 19). As light increases constantly from sunrise to full day, so the path of the saints always advances; but the way of the sinners becomes continually more dark and gloomy, till they know not where they go, and at length walk over a precipice.

* * *

An ardent desire of perfection is the first means that a Christian should adopt in order to acquire sanctity and to consecrate his whole being to God. As the sportsman, to hit a bird in flight, must take aim in advance of his prey, so a Christian, to make progress in virtue, should aspire to the highest degree of holiness which it is in his power to attain. "Who," says holy David, "will give me wings like a dove, and I will fly and be at rest" (Ps. liv, 7).

Holy desires are the blessed wings with which the saints burst every worldly tie, and fly to the mountain of perfection, where they find that peace which the world cannot give.

—*Henry: Manual of Self-Knowledge and Christian Perfection.*

* * *

Be you therefore perfect, as also your heavenly Father is perfect.

—*Matt. v, 48.*

* * *

Brethren, rejoice, be perfect, take exhortation, be of one mind, have peace; and the God of peace and of love shall be with you.
—*2 Cor. xiii, II.*

The Wings of Simplicity and Purity

The author of *The Imitation* says: "By two wings is man lifted above earthly things, namely, by simplicity and purity. Simplicity must be in the intention, purity in the affection. Simplicity aimeth at God, purity apprehendeth Him and tasteth Him. No good work will be a hindrance to thee provided thou be free interiorly from all inordinate affection. If thou aim at and seek after nothing else but the will of God and thy neighbor's benefit, then shalt thou enjoy interior liberty. If only thy heart were right, then every created thing would be to thee a mirror of life and a book of holy teaching. There is no creature so little and so vile that it showeth not forth the goodness of God."

"All men are vain, in whom there is not the knowledge of God: and who by these good things that are seen could not understand Him that is, neither by attending to the works have acknowledged who was the workman.

. . . With whose beauty, if they, being delighted, took them to be gods: let them know how much the Lord of them is more beautiful than they: for the first author of beauty made all those things.

Oh, if they admired their power and their effects, let them understand by them, that He that made them is mightier than they:

For by the greatness of the beauty, and of the creature, the Creator of them may be seen, so as to be known thereby" (Wis. xiii, 1, 3-5).

"The firmament on high is His beauty, the beauty of heaven with its glorious show.

The sun when he appeareth showing forth at his rising, an admirable instrument, the work of the most High. . . .

The glory of the stars is the beauty of heaven; the Lord enlighteneth the world on high. . . .

Look upon the rainbow, and bless Him that made it: it is very beautiful in its brightness.

It encompasseth the heaven about with the circle of its glory, the hands of the most High have displayed it" (Ecclus. xliii, 1, 2, 10, 12, 13).

THE IDEAL OF CHRISTIAN PERFECTION

The ideal of Christian perfection is fully realized only in the God-Man Jesus Christ.

Jesus Christ alone was without sin or defect. The holiest of men grieve over their sins and imperfections. Christ, though most humble, was not conscious of sin. He manifested the practice of all virtues in His life in an heroic degree. His charity and filial devotion towards God were most perfect. His charity toward men was profound, universal, efficacious. He loved all—Jews, Samaritans, Gentiles, the children, the poor, the infirm, the afflicted, the just, the sinners. Even Judas is His "friend". His love never degenerated into weakness. To the deepest humility and meekness He united dignity, magnanimity, and the most perfect sincerity. His firmness remained unshaken even in the torture of His passion, wherein He displayed heroic patience, praying for His persecutors and recommending His soul to His Father (Garrigou-Lagrange).

—*Laux: A Course in Religion.*

THE LOVELINESS OF JESUS

The most conspicuous virtues of Our Saviour's public life are submission to the will of His heavenly Father, zeal for His Father's glory, unbounded charity toward His neighbor, meekness, humility, patience, forbearance with others' faults and weaknesses, kindness to sinners, and compassion toward the poor, the sick, and unfortunate. He strove to become "all to all"; He went about "doing good to all."

Unquestionably our blessed Saviour possessed a charming exterior, a fascinating personality, a sweetness of speech, a quiet dignity of deportment, a gentleness and modesty of manner, that gave Him a marvelous influence over old and young, over men, women, and children. "Thou art beautiful," says the Psalmist, "above the sons of men; grace is poured abroad in Thy lips; with Thy comeliness and Thy beauty, set out, proceed prosperously, and reign."

He spoke in simple language; yet all wondered at the words of grace that proceeded from His mouth. Why did His simple words convey such an impression? Because with the latent power of divine grace, the "goodness and kindness of God our Saviour hath appeared to all men, instructing us." He hated sin, but He was merciful to sinners. The Prophet Isaias said of Him that He would not be "sad nor troublesome." He had all His senses under control. His manner and His person were a reflection of the calm, the peace, the order that reigned within.

"He shall not contend, nor cry out, neither shall any man hear His voice in the streets. The bruised reed He shall not break, and smoking flax He shall not extinguish" (Matt. xii, 19, 20). Jesus is your Master, your Model. Contemplate the loveliness of Jesus, and then your own sweetness will be apparent, your own modesty will be known to all, and that modesty will edify others and preach a powerful sermon—that modesty will indicate the purity of your soul; it will also feed and nourish the spirit of interior recollection.

Let your modesty be known to all men.

—*Philipp. iv, 5.*

For the rest, brethren, whatsoever things are true, whatsoever modest, whatsoever just, whatsoever holy, whatsoever lovely, whatsoever of good fame, if there be any virtue, if any praise of discipline, think on these things.

—*Philipp. iv, 8.*

THE HABIT DOES NOT MAKE THE MONK

In spite of her high esteem for the religious life, the Church has ever held that there is no twofold ideal of perfection, one for the Religious and one for the Christian in the world: for both the measure of their love of God is the measure of their perfection. *Habitus non facit monachum.* The habit does not make the monk. "Habit and tonsure," says Thomas à Kempis, "profit little; but change of heart and perfect mortification of the passions make a true monk." Many men and women in the world have attained as high a degree of sanctity as those who have spent their lives in convents and monasteries. Great saints of God have been found, and are still found, in every state and condition of life.

—*Laux: A Course in Religion.*

* * *

Not every one that saith to me, Lord, Lord, shall enter into the kingdom of heaven: but he that doth the will of my Father who is in heaven, he shall enter into the kingdom of heaven.

—*Matt. vii, 21.*

Now this I say: He who soweth sparingly, shall also reap sparingly: and he who soweth in blessings, shall also reap blessings.

Every one as he hath determined in his heart, not with sadness, or of necessity: for God loveth a cheerful giver.
—*2 Cor. ix, 6, 7.*

* * *

And do ye all things without murmurings and hesitations;

That you may be blameless and sincere children of God, without reproof, in the midst of a crooked and perverse generation; among whom you shine as lights in the world.
—*Philipp. ii, 14, 15.*

Blessed Are They That Suffer Persecution for Justice' Sake

Under the term persecution are comprehended all kinds of injuries, afflictions and inconveniences, in relation to fortune, honor, or life. These are caused by the devil or his ministers, sometimes, also, by mistake (God so permitting), by the just themselves. They are suffered for justice' sake, when they are borne with patience and accompanied with the exercise of virtue, and in compliance with our duty toward God and man. They ought not to be suffered with patience only, but with joy at the greatness of the reward; therefore, St. Peter says, "Let none of you suffer as a murderer, or a thief, or a railer, or as coveting the goods of others, but if as a Christian, let him not be ashamed, but let him glorify God in that name" (1 Peter iv, 15).

Christ suffered all kinds of injuries and inconveniences in His honor, in His goods, and in His person, for a cause, which on His part was perfectly just. He suffered in consequence of His publishing His divine law and endeavoring to bring men back again from vice and folly, into the way of their eternal salvation.

Therefore, "Look and make it according to the pattern" (Ex. xxv, 40).

The reward attached to the suffering for justice' sake is no less than "the kingdom of heaven." When you suffer, then, with joy and patience, "Rejoice and be exceeding glad, because your reward is very great in heaven." Ponder deeply, therefore, the greatness of the reward, and the truth of the apostolic oracle. "The sufferings of this present time are not worthy to be compared with the glory to come, that shall be revealed in us" (Rom. viii, 18).

* * *

And though in the sight of men they suffered torments, their hope is full of immortality.

Afflicted in few things, in many they shall be well rewarded: because God hath tried them, and found them worthy of himself—Wis. iii. 4. 5.

* * *

Patience

As the lord of men, Jesus Christ became their teacher, and He exhorts us to take up our daily cross, and to follow Him with patience.

Severe to Himself, He is gentle, mild, and forbearing to all others. His meekness is the beautiful flower, His peacefulness the sweet fruit of His patience. His doctrine is doubted and disputed; He is charged with being an impostor; He is called a blasphemer; His wonderful works are ascribed to the devil; His adversaries gnash their teeth, burn with rage, and are prepared to stone Him. Yet His equanimity is unmoved, His meek demeanor is not altered, the calmness of His peace undergoes no change. Resting on His union with His Father, the ground of His invincible strength, His divine fortitude is tried at every point, and at every point His patience is invincible.

—Ullathorne.

The patient man is better than the valiant: and he that ruleth his spirit, than he that taketh cities.

—Prov. xvi, 92.

* * *

Bearing in union with His passion the little humiliations, rebuffs, and trials of everyday life brings us wonderfully near to Our Lord and to sanctity.

The spiritual life is the sweetest and happiest thing in the world—to love God and be loved by Him.

To do His will is to love Him.

His will is to be found in the ordinary little things of every minute.

We please Him and win His love in the same way as we please and win an earthly friend.

There are very few invariable rules in the spiritual life, but this is one: Pray in the way that you like best.

—Fr. Considine, S.J.

* * *

A sacrifice to God is an afflicted spirit: a contrite and humbled heart, O God, thou wilt not despise.

—Ps. l, 19.

* * *

The Lord is the keeper of little ones.

—Ps. cxiv, 6.

The greater thou art, the more humble thyself in all things, and thou shalt find grace before God:

For great is the power of God alone, and He is honored by the humble.

—Ecclus. iii, 20, 21.

SELF-LOVE

Jesus said to His disciples: "If any man will come after Me, let him deny himself, take up His cross, and follow Me" (Matt. xvi, 24). The capital enemy of the love of God, and of all our good—especially of resignation and conformity—of our will to the will of God, is the vice of self-love, that is to say, a disorderly inclination to gratify and please ourselves, which is the unhappy consequence of the corruption of man by sin, and the fruitful parent of all our evils. Our vices and passions spring from this poisonous root; the seven capital sins are but so many branches of this inordinate inclination to ourselves. Take away self-love, and you will shut up all the avenues of hell, and establish everywhere the reign of the love of God, and a most blessed heaven upon earth. Hence the virtue of *self-denial*, the business of which is to suppress and root out this evil of self-love, is one of the most necessary of all Christian virtues, and must ever go hand in hand with the great virtue of conformity to the will of God, which can never take root in our souls as long as we are unhappily attached to our own wills and fond of gratifying our own inclinations. Hence, the very first condition the Son of God requires of all that would be His disciples is to deny themselves (Matt. xvi, 24). This self-denial is the great lesson He came down from heaven to teach. Happy we, if by His grace we can but effectually learn it in practice.

* * *

He that taketh not up his cross, and followeth Me, is not worthy of Me.

—*Matt. x, 38.*

Mortification

This virtue of self-denial is usually called mortification from a word signifying "slaying" or "putting to death": inasmuch as by this continual fighting against ourselves and against our own corrupt inclinations and passions, we put to death, as it were, and crucify the old man of corruption (Rom. vi, 6), with his vices and sins (according to that of the Apostle (Gal. v, 24), that they that are of Christ have crucified their flesh with its vices and concupiscences), and so die to ourselves, that we may put on the new man, Jesus Christ, and live in such manner to Him as to be able to say with the same Apostle, "I live now, not I, but Christ liveth in me" (Gal. ii, 20). See, my soul, what this virtue of mortification means which is much talked of and but little understood, and less practised, and yet no virtue is more necessary for our true welfare.

* * *

They that have found out so easy a way to heaven, as to take no thought, but make merry, nor take no penance at all, but sit cock-a-hoop and fill in all the cups at once, and then let Christ's Passion pay for all the shot, I am not he that will envy their good hap.

We must not look to go to heaven on feather beds; that is not the way, for Our Lord Himself went thither with great pain; and the servant must not look to be in better case than his master.

—*St. Thomas More.*

* * *

Whosoever doth not carry his cross, and come after Me, can not be My disciple.

—*Luke xiv, 27.*

THE DEVIL, THE WORLD, AND THE FLESH

The flesh with its passions and lusts is always reckoned by divines amongst the three great enemies of the soul, and is indeed of all the three by far the most dangerous enemy, because the world and the devil, with all their suggestions, would not easily draw us into sin and hell if our own flesh, that is, our corrupt inclinations and passions, did not pave the way and furnish them with the arms with which they fight against us. The world and the devil besiege us from without, but could never force their way into the soul if our own evil inclination did not hold a correspondence with them and open the gates of the soul to let them in.

Conclude, if thou desirest to overcome the world and the devil, to make it thy business to subdue the flesh and to bring it under subjection by self-denials and mortifications.

* * *

Believe me, the mortification of the senses—of the sight, the hearing, the tongue—is more beneficial than to wear a chain of iron and the hair-shirt.

—*St. Francis of Sales.*

* * *

When St. Francis Borgia heard it said of anyone, "He is a saint," he would reply: "He will be a saint if he constantly mortify himself."

* * *

If you live according to the flesh, you shall die: but if by the Spirit you mortify the deeds of the flesh, you shall live.
—*Rom. viii, 13.*

Know you not that they that run in the race, all run indeed, but one receiveth the prize? So run that you may obtain.

And every one that striveth for the mastery, refraineth himself from all things: and they indeed that they may receive a corruptible crown; but we an incorruptible one.
—*1 Cor. ix, 24, 25.*

St. Francis De Sales On Mortification

Blessed Francis was no great friend of unusual mortifications, and did not wish them to be practised except in the pressing necessity of violent temptations.

With regard to the various kinds of mortification, that which is inward and hidden is far more excellent than that which is exterior, the former not being compatible, as is the latter, with hypocrisy, vanity, or indiscretion.

Again, those mortifications which come upon us from without, either directly from God or through men by His permission, are always superior to those which depend upon our own choice and which are the offspring of our will.

Many, however, find here a stumbling block, being very eager to embrace mortifications suggested by their own inclinations, which, after all, however apparently severe, are really easy because they are what nature itself wants.

On the other hand, mortifications which come to them from without and through others, however light they may be, they find insupportable. For example, a person will eagerly make use of disciplines, hair-shirts, and fasting, and yet will be so tender of his reputation that, if once in a way laughed at or spoken against, he will become almost beside himself, robbed of his rest and even sometimes of his reason, and will perhaps in the end be driven to the most deplorable extremities.

Another will give alms liberally and make magnificent foundations for the relief of the poor and sick, but will groan and tremble with fear when himself threatened with infirmity or sickness, however slightly; and upon experiencing the least possible bodily pain, will give vent to interminable lamentations.

In proportion as people are more or less attached to honors, gain, or mere pleasures, they bear with less or more patience the hindrances to them; nor do the majority of men seriously consider that it is the hand of God which gives and which takes away, which kills and which makes alive, which exalts and which casts down, as it pleases Him.

* * *

I beseech you therefore, brethren, by the mercy of God, that you present your bodies a living sacrifice, holy pleasing unto God, your reasonable service.

—*Rom. xii, i.*

But One Thing Is Necessary

Reflect upon these words of our Saviour: *"Thou art careful and art troubled about many things: But one thing is necessary"* (Luke x, 41, 42).

It is not difficult to discern what this one thing necessary is. What else can it be but the dedication of ourselves to the love and service of our God in order that we may secure the eternal salvation of our souls.

"Vanity of vanities and all is vanity but to love and serve God alone" (*Imitation*). Alas! what a multiplicity of cares and anxieties about worldly affairs and empty vanities is apt to take up our whole mind and heart! What a variety of amusements distract our thoughts! In what a dissipation do we generally live! How little do we think of God and of things that count for eternity!

To love and to serve God! This is our real business, our only business; this is the business for which alone we came into the world. Whatever our employment or calling be in the world, it must be ever subordinate to this great business. All our thoughts, words, and deeds should ever tend to God and to our eternal salvation.

Whatsoever has no tendency to the one thing necessary is idle and vain. "What doth it profit a man if he gain the whole world, and lose his own soul?" (Matt. xvi, 26).

* * *

"Seek ye first the kingdom of God and His justice, and all these things shall be added unto you."

—Matt. vi, 33.

The Mind of Christ

There are found in the Epistles of St. Paul many outbursts of most astounding eloquence, above all in treating of the life and work of our Blessed Lord. His words there betray the fire of divine love which burned within his breast. One of these passages occurs in the second chapter of the Epistle to the Philippians (vv, 5-11), in which he describes for us the mind of Christ our Lord, which also is to be our mind and aim:

"Let this mind be in you, which was also in Christ Jesus: Who being in the form of God thought it not robbery to be equal with

God: But emptied Himself, taking the form of a servant, being made in the likeness of men, and in habit found as a man. He humbled Himself, becoming obedient unto death, even to the death of the Cross: For which cause God also hath exalted Him, and hath given Him a name which is above all names: That in the name of Jesus every knee should bow, of those that are in heaven, on earth, and under the earth: And that every tongue should confess that the Lord Jesus Christ is in the glory of God the Father."

This, then, is the "mind of Christ"; in poverty and labors from His youth, with nowhere to lay His head, a man of sorrows, looking for one to comfort Him and finding none, deserted by His own, called a seducer, rejected in favor of a robber and a murderer, crucified between two thieves, obedient unto death, He rose again, the Lord of life, mighty in battle, death having now no more dominion over Him; He has led captivity captive; He has established a kingdom of which there shall be no end, and, ascending on high at the uplifting of the eternal gates, He sitteth at the right hand of the Father, whence He shall come in power and majesty to judge the world and render to every man according to his works.

Thus has He "made all things new." By such means it is that the Fatherhood of God has been brought home to men, that we have been made the sons of God, and enabled to cry "Abba, Father." Thus have we been made "partakers of the Divine Nature," "joint heirs with Christ," and "temples of God," hoping "to see the good things of the Lord in the land of the living," hoping to "see God as He is," "face to face," for evermore.

Indeed God's ways are not as man's. The weak things are God's choice to confound the strong. Great and bountiful as is the purpose and work of Christ, it is brought about by means the most strange, the most contrary to the dictates of human wisdom. All rich, our Lord became poor; all powerful, He sank beneath His load; all strong, He sat down weary by the well; all wise, He was called mad and clad in the garment of a fool; the Lord of all, He humbled Himself, and "is in the midst of us as He that serveth." To the world it is folly and a stumbling-block, mere waste of time; but it is "the mind of Christ," and in it are contained those generative forces by which, and by which alone, the kingdom of Christ is established and propagated, by which souls are made "full of grace" and "enabled to walk worthy of their high vocation." For "this mind which was in Christ Jesus must also be in us." "The servant is not above his Lord; it is sufficient that he be as his Lord."

And if Our Lord, in reviewing His work and the spirit in which it had been carried out, could say, "Ought not Christ to have suffered and so enter into His glory?" surely we must say "Ought not the disciples of Christ to suffer, and so enter into their glory?" There is much in that "ought" and in that "so." Surely we must "take His yoke upon us," and "learn of Him," that "our meat be the will of Him that sent us." We must "fall into the ground and die, that we remain not alone, but bring forth much fruit." "The charity of Christ presseth us." His glorious example presseth us to take to heart the great lessons which are our passport to His kingdom. God's road to victory must be ours also. We cannot possibly make one for ourselves. "*Per crucem ad lucem*; no cross, no crown"; it is the old law; "let this mind be in us, for it was first in Christ Jesus."

It is incumbent upon all to breathe this spirit and practise these truths. To some the occasions for their exercise are more plentiful and extensive than to others. The sick and desolate are especially rich in chances of learning and deriving fruit from this counsel.

Blessed are they if they appreciate their chances and welcome the lesson, turning it to the glory of God and the good of souls. Foolish are they if they resent the chalice as too bitter for them, and, closing their eyes to light, suffer not "the mind which was in Christ Jesus," their Lord and Friend, to be in them also.

"Lead me, O Lord, in the eternal way. Show Thy ways to me and teach me Thy paths. If I have erred, teach Thou me. Send forth Thy light and Thy truth. They shall conduct me and bring me unto Thy holy hill and into Thy tabernacle."

—Eaton: One Hundred Readings for the Sick.

* * *

Take up My yoke upon you, and learn of Me, because I am meek, and humble of heart: and you shall find rest to your souls.
—Matt. xi, 29.

* * *

The disciple is not above his master: but every one shall be perfect, if he be as his master.
—Luke vi, 40.

* * *

For I have given you an example, that as I have done to you, so you do also.
—John xiii, 15.

* * *

Unto this are you called: because Christ also suffered for us, leaving you an example, that you should follow His steps.
—Peter ii, 21.

It Is Necessary That You Should Be Conformed to the Image and Likeness of Jesus Christ

In several of his Epistles to the first Christians, St. Paul speaks of the necessity of conformity with Jesus Christ as a condition for obtaining the crown of eternal glory. He tells them that everyone who is predestined for heaven must first be transformed into the image and likeness of the Son of God. The heavenly Father will receive as His child him only in whom He can trace the lineaments of His eternal Son, and of whom He can testify as He testified of Him on Mount Tabor: "This is My beloved Son, in Whom I am well pleased."

But Jesus Christ was a Man of sorrows. From the very first moment of His earthly life down to His last breath on the cross, He suffered incessantly both in His soul and in His body. His actual passion lasted only a few hours, it is true; but its anticipation, which included the clearest foreknowledge of its minutest details, accompanied Him all through life and never left Him without suffering, no, not for a single moment.

Listen to His own words: "If anyone will come after Me, let him deny himself, take up his cross daily, and follow Me. For whosoever shall save his life, shall lose it; and he that will lose his life for My sake, shall save it. He that taketh up not his cross and followeth Me, is not worthy of Me." Hear how St. Paul teaches the same doctrine. "You have received the Spirit of adoption of sons, whereby we cry: Abba (i.e., Father)! For the Spirit Himself giveth testimony to our spirit that we are the sons of God. And if sons, heirs also; heirs indeed of God and joint-heirs with Christ; yet so if we suffer with Him that we may also be glorified with Him."

Consequently, if you are weighed down by crosses, though you have long tried to lead a life of piety and virtue and, therefore, imagine that you ought to be entirely free from such trials, remember that the heavenly Artist is at work transforming you by slow degrees into a perfect image of Jesus Christ.

If you keep these truths always in mind, they will strengthen and greatly encourage you when tempted to impatience or despondency. Never forget that *"You shall reign with Christ in heaven only if you suffer with Him here on earth."*
—Rev. F. J. Remler, C.M.: *Why Must I Suffer?*
(Franciscan Herald Press).

* * *

If we suffer, we shall also reign with Him.
—*2 Tim. ii, 12.*

The Sufferings of Christ

All the saints cherished a tender devotion toward Jesus Christ in His Passion. By the sufferings of Christ it is made known how much God loved man. Our Saviour would win our love by His sorrows and sufferings in our behalf. "Greater love than this no man hath, that a man lay down his life for his friends" (John xv, 13). "And I, if I be lifted up from the earth, will draw all things to Myself" (John xii, 32).

Meditation on the Passion has been the grand occupation of all holy souls. We can not make too much of the stupendous fact that Christ suffered—and suffered all His life—in every variety of pain and anguish beyond what it was possible for mere mortal men to suffer. Suffering in this exercise of her divine and austere mission, was waiting for Him when He set His foot upon the earth. She stood beside the crib at Bethlehem, and accompanied Him in the wanderings of His infancy. She dwelt within the walls of the holy house, cherished by Jesus, Mary, and Joseph. When

He went forth upon His Father's business, she trod the ways of Judea and Galilee by His side, and led Him by the hand to toil, to contempt, to ingratitude, to cold, and hunger, and watching. She caused Him to feel the sorrows of His Mother. She let Him taste the bitterness of being disowned by the high and by the lowly, rejected by His own people, distrusted by the little children. She wrung from Him, in the garden, that cry of anguish prophesied long before: "Save me, O God, for the waters have broken in even upon my soul!" (Ps. lxviii, i). She beckoned Him to the pretorium, and to the mockery and horror of the crowning with thorns. She laid the cross upon His bleeding shoulders, and went before Him on the road to Calvary. Then she stood still on the mountain of myrrh and the hill of frankincense, where bitterness was to be supreme and sacrifice was to go up to the heavens; she stood still, and pointed to the cross and the nails; and He said: "Behold, I come!" And when the cross had been lifted up, suffering, for yet three hours, lingered in the silence of the darkness; for yet three hours—and then her mission was at an end; and, as when a dark cloud breaks and the rains stream upon the earth, suffering, since that day, has fallen on men and women in every age and over all the world, and every drop has been full of the fragrance of the cross.

The passion of our Lord and Saviour, therefore, is intended to unite our hearts to His in that easy and sweet worship which is founded upon compassion.

Mental prayer should often take the passion for its subject; we should follow with loving care each step of Him Who bore our sorrows, from the Supper even to Calvary.

There is nothing that happens in which the heart will not be directed, profited, and lifted up by connecting it with the passion. Especially will this be found true in the commonest of all the events of a life on earth—hardship, trouble, and sorrow. When these things come upon us, there is no solid comfort or support unless we leave self and creatures, and turn to God. To resist, to fret, to bewail ourselves, to give way to impatience, to seek consolation in sin or imperfection, to indulge in murmuring or in dissipation of spirit—these things palliate trouble; but they leave it rooted in the soul. Only one thing plucks it out, and that is to turn with it to Christ. My Lord and my Master, we may say to Him, Thou didst suffer and suffer far more than this. To Thee, suffering was familiar; Thou didst choose it for Thy lot and Thy inheritance—and I, I dread it and refuse it! By Thy loving acceptance of pain, give me the courage to accept all that I have to suffer!

—Bishop Medley.

* * *

My brethren, count it all joy, when you shall fall into divers temptations;

Knowing that the trying of your faith worketh patience.

And patience hath a perfect work; that you may be perfect and entire, failing in nothing.

—James i, 2-4.

* * *

Take, my brethren, for an example of suffering evil, of labor and patience, the prophets, who spoke in the name of the Lord.

Behold, we account them blessed who have endured. You have heard of the patience of Job, and you have seen the end of the Lord, that the Lord is merciful and compassionate.

—James v, 10, 11.

* * *

Wait on God with patience: join thyself to God, and endure, that thy life may be increased in the latter end.

Take all that shall be brought upon thee: and in thy sorrow endure, and in thy humiliation keep patience.

For gold and silver are tried in the fire, but acceptable men in the furnace of humiliation.

—Ecclus. ii, 3-5.

PART III.
THE PASSION AND DEATH OF OUR LORD

The Way of the Cross

"After they had mocked Him, they took off the cloak from Him, and put on Him His own garments, and led Him away to crucify Him" (Matt. xxvii, 31).

"And bearing His own cross He went forth to that place which is called Calvary, but in Hebrew Golgotha.

"Where they crucified him, and with him two others, one on each side, and Jesus in the midst.

"And Pilate wrote a title also: and he put it upon the cross. And the writing was: Jesus of Nazareth, the King of the Jews.

"This title therefore many of the Jews did read: because the place where Jesus was crucified was nigh to the city. And it was written in Hebrew, in Greek, and in Latin.

"Then the chief priests of the Jews said to Pilate: Write not: The King of the Jews. But that he said: I am the King of the Jews.

"Pilate answered: What I have written, I have written" (John xix, 17-22).

* * *

A man condemned to crucifixion was made to bear his cross to the place of execution, that is, the transverse beam of it; for the upright post was either erected beforehand or carried thither on a cart. This crossbeam was a stout piece of timber some eight feet long, a heavy load for one so exhausted as Our Lord was. He receives it in gladness of heart; for has He not been looking forward to it all His life long? The thought of it in the garden filled Him with terror; but "love is strong as death" (Cant, viii, 6). "Perfect charity casteth out fear" (1 John iv, 18). The two thieves are also loaded with their crosses and the procession sets forth. A cart leads the way carrying the ladders and the three long beams; then come the executioners with ropes and heavy hammers and huge nails, which are to be driven with those hammers into human flesh, and last of all the three victims. But Jesus has gone but a few paces when He stumbles and falls. The wood is lifted from His shoulder, and He is raised and set on His feet.

Via Crucis

The path of life is rough and stony. Sharp flints and hidden thorns are thickly strewn upon its surface, wounding our weary feet as we toil ever onward and upward toward our heavenly home. Does our courage fail, do our hearts grow faint? Do our aching eyes look sadly upon that broad and tempting way, so bright, so pleasant, so attractive to our senses—but which we know would lead us on to destruction? Then, turn to Christ as He hangs upon the cruel gibbet with outstretched arms and bleeding hands. *Passio Christi, conforta me.* Passion of Christ strengthen me, for the way is long and weary: comfort me as I fight my way along the path of life safely to the haven of Thy Sacred Heart; comfort me in that last dread hour of summons to Thy feet.

—*William Doyle, S.J.*

* * *

Precious in the sight of the Lord is the death of His saints.
—*Ps. cxv, 15.*

Why Should I Suffer? What Have I Done?

There are many who say, "Why should I suffer? What have I done?" When I hear remarks of that kind I answer: "Are you a Christian man—a follower of Him Who said, 'Deny yourselves, take up your cross, and follow Me'?" Then take up your cross bravely, patiently, and gladly.

Suffering is needed in this world in order that we may develop character. If borne in conformity to the will of God, it brings out all that is good in us, for until we meet with trouble and trial and temptation, sadness, sickness, and sorrow, we have not put forth our whole powers to account. God sends us suffering that its purging fires may purify and make beautiful the Christian soul, and no child of God has ever passed through the golden gate without having shed tears in this land of exile. But, remember, it will be when we reach that land where death and sorrow shall be no more, and not before, that God will wipe away all tears from our eyes. It is as though He would tell us in His own gentle, sweet, and suggestive way that till we reach that life of eternal happiness, tears must furrow our cheeks, and sorrow must be with us, and through a mist of tears, like the haze on the river, the cloud on the mountain, the dew on the heather, we must look up to our home in heaven.

Only be faithful to your mission in life, be up and doing, true to yourselves, loving to your God. Then you will look back upon the trials and troubles, the sickness and the sadness of your earthly pilgrimage, as leaders of armies look back upon their struggles and wounds after the shouts of victory proclaim the battle won.

—*Bernard Vaughan, S.J.*

* * *

Blessed is the man that endureth temptation; for when he hath been proved, he shall receive the crown of life, which God hath promised to them that love Him.

—*James i, 12.*

The Love of Jesus Crucified

Good Catholics will not forget the love of Jesus crucified. They will take care that the image of their crucified Saviour is in a prominent place in their house; they will carry a crucifix with them; they will frequently perform some devotion in honor of the wounds of Jesus, such as saying five times, Glory be to the Father, etc., in honor of the wounds in the sacred hands and feet and side of our divine Lord; they will sometimes make the Way of the Cross, remembering that all that is necessary is to pass from station to station and reflect a little on the passion; above all, they will not fail on Fridays faithfully to observe and willingly to accept the mortification of abstinence from flesh meat which the Church imposes on her children as an act of gratitude to Jesus Christ Who suffered and died for them on that day.

—*C. McNeiry, C.SS.R.*

* * *

With Christ I am nailed to the cross.

—*Gal. ii, 19.*

* * *

The hearts of the saints, like sea-shells, murmur of the Passion evermore.

—*Fr. Faber.*

Resolve to meditate daily on the Passion of Jesus Christ, and to practice the virtues He has taught us in His sufferings. *Who is He that suffers?* Viewing the Passion as a whole, ask yourself this question: Who is He that suffers?

1. The Lamb without spot, "who did not sin, neither was guile found in His mouth" (1 Pet. ii, 22), the Holy of Holies, whom His very executioners acknowledge to be holy and the Son of God.

2. That Jesus of Nazareth who "went about doing good and healing all that were oppressed by the devil" (Acts x, 38). This is the return He meets with: "They repaid Me evil for good" (Ps. xxxiv, 12).

3. The Good Shepherd, the Good Samaritan, the Lover of men.

What did He suffer? Most cruel bodily torture. If your crucifix represented Christ as He really looked you would sicken at the sight; and yet this mangled body is but the title-page to the book of the passion; the anguish of His soul was something far more terrible.

—*Fr. Barraud's Meditations.*

* * *

I lay down My life for My sheep.

—*John x, 15.*

AT WHOSE HANDS DID HE SUFFER?

At the hands of His own people. "Thy own nation," said Pilate, "and the chief priests have delivered Thee up to me. What hast

Thou done?" (John xviii, 35). What, indeed? The land was ringing with the miracles of His mercy; yet the entire people rose against Him. "And they shall say to Him: What are these wounds in the midst of Thy hands? And He shall say: With these I was wounded in the house of them that loved Me" (Zach. xiii, 6).

For whose sins did He suffer?

For the sins of them who crucified Him, for my sins. "He loved me and delivered Himself for me" (Gal. ii, 20).

How Did He Suffer?

1. With unruffled patience, neither reproaching His persecutors nor defending Himself. "Who, when He was reviled, did not revile; when He suffered, He threatened not; but delivered Himself to him that judged Him unjustly" (1 Peter ii, 23). "He shall be led as a sheep to the slaughter, and shall be dumb as a lamb before his shearer, and He shall not open His mouth" (Is. liii, 71).

2. *With divine love.* "I am the Good Shepherd. The Good Shepherd giveth His life for His sheep" (John x, 11). "I have a baptism wherewith I am to be baptized; and how am I straitened until it be accomplished?" (Luke xii, 50).

* * *

The charity of Christ presseth us: judging this, that if one died for all, then all were dead.

And Christ died for all; that they also who live, may not now live to themselves, but unto Him who died for them, and rose again.

—*2 Cor. v, 14, 15.*

THE DREAM OF THE HOLY CHILD

You may have seen a picture of the Babe of Bethlehem asleep in the manger, while above His head moves the sad procession in which He is carrying His cross to Calvary. The dream of the Holy Child reminds us of a deep and touching truth. From the first moment of His life all the anguish of His coming passion was present to our Saviour; waking or sleeping He never lost sight of it. He looked forward to it with dread indeed and yet with most earnest longing.

To me the cross is terrible—I can not help that; yet if I love Jesus Christ ever so little I shall try to bear it cheerfully for His dear sake.

"The whole life of Christ was a cross and a martyrdom, and dost thou seek for thyself rest and joy?"

—*Thomas à Kempis.*

* * *

"Unto you it is given for Christ, not only to believe in Him, but also to suffer for Him."

—*Philipp. i, 29.*

* * *

OUR LORD FORETOLD HIS PASSION TO HIS DISCIPLES

Our Saviour foretold His passion several times; but just before His death, He did this with greater distinctness than ever (Mark x).

"They were in the way going up to Jerusalem; and Jesus went before them, and following they were afraid." The haste our Saviour made on this last journey to Jerusalem shows how eager He was to begin His passion. It filled His apostles with fear because they knew His enemies were waiting for Him. And then He scares them still more by foretelling in detail the sufferings He is to undergo: "Behold, we go up to Jerusalem, and the Son of man shall be betrayed to the chief priests and to the scribes and ancients, and they shall condemn Him to death and shall deliver Him to the Gentiles, and they shall mock Him and spit on Him and scourge Him and kill Him; and the third day He shall rise again."

Until the very last night before His Passion, there was nothing in Our Lord's manner to cause His disciples any serious alarm. The preaching and the miracles go on to the very end. There is no tremor in their Master's voice, no trouble in His eyes, no pallor on His cheek. He is just the same as ever with the people, just the same with them. He does nothing to avert the blow that hangs over Him. His hour has come and He is there to meet it, quiet, self-possessed, serenely calm.

Again, there is no fretfulness, such as we often show when we have anything to suffer, but on the contrary a most marvelous sweetness. He is severe, indeed, toward the pharisees, for they were hypocrites; but to the people how kind He is! We see Him gathering the little children about Him, embracing and blessing them, weeping over the Holy City, defending those who sang *"Hosanna,"* commending the widow's mite, defending Magdalen; and to the traitor Judas how patient, how gentle He is! Not one thought for Himself; all His care is for us.

* * *

You call Me Master and Lord. And you say well; for so I am. I have given you an example, that as I have done to you, so you do also.

—*John xiii, 13, 15.*

Hosannas

Christ rode upon an ass from Bethania to Jerusalem, and the multitude that went before and that followed cried, saying: "Hosanna to the Son of David! Blessed is He that cometh in the name of the Lord. Hosanna in the highest!"

And when He drew near, seeing the city, He wept over it, saying: "If thou hadst known, and that is this thy day, the things that are to thy peace; but now they are hidden from thy eyes."

Jesus knows that within a few short days the *"Hosannas"* of these children will be changed into the execrations of their fathers. That terrible cry even now sounds in His ears: "His blood be upon us and upon our children," these very children whose innocent lips are now chanting the hymn of praise. May God save me from the curse of a hardened heart and give me grace to know the day of my visitation.

What a lesson we have here of the falsehood and fickleness of this world and the folly of setting one's hopes on it! It is ready at any moment to turn round on us, to cast us off, to laugh at our affliction. So long as a man is rich and prosperous he is worshipped wherever he goes; every one stands cap in hand to receive him; but let him fall into poverty—then how soon his trencher friends will drop away! They have shared his sunshine gladly enough; but they hid from him in foul weather. Semei threw stones at David when he was fleeing from Absalom; when he returned in triumph he went to meet him and do him honor. The lesson is as old as the hills; yet every man and woman has to learn it by bitter experience. "O ye sons of men, how long will you be dull of heart? Why do you love vanity, and seek after lying?" (Is. iv, 3).

Give me grace, O my God, to despise the world and to serve Thee alone.

LESSONS OF OUR LORD ON THE EVE OF HIS PASSION

Love of Himself is the first lesson. "As the Father hath loved Me I also have loved you. Abide in My love." "The Father Himself hath loved you because you have loved Me." Christ, therefore, is the bond of union between God and man; for God must love those who love His Son, and the more they love His beloved the greater His love for them.

"If you love Me keep My commandments." This shows how we are to prove our love for Christ and provides a sure test of the depth and sincerity of our love; for we can not bear to displease those who are really dear to us.

"If you keep My commandments you shall abide in My love, as I also have kept My Father's commandments and do abide in His love."

The second lesson is love of our neighbor.—"A new commandment I give unto you, that you love one another." He calls it with good reason a new commandment; for it goes far beyond the prescription of the old law, "Thou shalt love thy friend as thyself" (Lev. xix, 18). Our Lord would have us love not our friends only, but our enemies, a lesson He has taught in the parable of the Good Samaritan and was to enforce again on the cross by His prayer for them that crucified Him.

* * *

You have heard that it hath been said, Thou shalt love thy neighbor, and hate thy enemy.

But I say to you. Love your enemies: do good to them that hate you: and pray for them that persecute and calumniate you:

That you may be the children of your Father who is in heaven, who maketh his sun to rise upon the good and bad, and raineth upon the just and the unjust.

For if you love them that love you, what reward shall you have? do not even the publicans this?

And if you salute your brethren only, what do you more? do not also the heathens this?

—Matt. v, 43-47.

* * *

And if you love them that love you, what thanks are to you? for sinners also love those that love them.

And if you do good to them who do good to you, hoping for nothing thereby: and your reward shall be great, and you shall be the sons of the Highest; for he is kind to the unthankful, and to the evil.

—Luke vi, 32, 33, 35.

Remember Me!

Every tabernacle is surmounted by a cross, because the Blessed Sacrament is a memorial of Our Lord's Passion and death. "As often as ye shall eat this bread and drink this chalice, ye shall show forth the death of the Lord until He come."

Why? Because it was given as a parting gift on the eve of the Passion, and because it contains our Lord and perpetuates Him as the Victim of the Cross.

In the first place it was given as a parting gift. Let us recall the touching episode of the Last Supper. Jesus and His apostles are seated at the table for the celebration of the Paschal solemnity. It is the last meal they are to take together, for He is about to leave them. They have lived in His company for almost three years. He has been the kindest of masters and truest of friends, and now He is to part from them. Their hearts are filled with sorrow. Our Lord is sorrowful too. He knows how they will miss Him. He knows their weakness. "You shall all be scandalized in Me," He says to them. Every farewell makes a pathetic scene. He is going to meet death; tomorrow evening at the same hour He will be in His grave, and they will have shamefully forsaken Him; their head and chief will have even thrice denied Him. Jesus foresees all this, yet He will not cast them off. "Having loved His own, He loved them unto the end." Even in those last hours of His life, when His soul is sorrowful unto death, He will give them a token of His undying love. He will compel them to remember Him. A death-bed gift is always a precious gift, more especially if it be a souvenir to which the heart of the dying one clings and around which entwine all the tenderest memories of the dear departed one.

And so the Divine Master says to His disciples: "I am with you all days even to the consummation of ages." His presence amongst us is the gift He is about to confer upon His children. He is to die, and yet to remain living amid these scenes until the end of time.

Hearken to His words: "I am the living Bread that came down from heaven. . . . Whosoever eateth Me the same shall live by Me. . . . Take ye and eat, this is My Body. Drink ye all of this, for this is My Blood." And then He adds: "Do this; do as you have seen Me do. You also take bread and wine and consecrate them into My Flesh and My Blood, and do this in memory of Me."

Dear Lord, blessed be Thy Holy Name! This very morning we have gathered at Thy Banquet. Thou hast fed us as Thou didst feed Thy apostles and disciples, and Thou art still as truly, really, and substantially present here, as Thou wert that blessed night with Thy chosen ones in Jerusalem's "upper room."

The Blessed Eucharist is a Memorial because it is the parting gift of our Lord to the apostles and to us. But it is also a Memorial because it contains our Lord as the Victim of the Cross; it perpetuates Him, as it were, in that state.

When we look at this Blessed Sacrament, let us recall that pathetic word of our Lord, "Remember Me!" Let us reflect that it is a Memorial of the greatest sorrow men ever witnessed, a Memorial of the greatest pain a creature on earth ever endured, a Memorial of the tenderest, most faithful, most unselfish, most heroic love the world shall ever know—the last gift of a Heart that fears to be forgotten. Lord, we will remember Thee! "May my tongue cleave to the roof of my mouth, and my hand wither and rot away, if I should ever forget Thee!"

—*Brinkmeyer: Short Conferences on the Sacred Heart of Jesus (Adapted).*

* * *

Be ye therefore followers of God, as most dear children;

And walk in love, as Christ also hath loved us, and hath delivered Himself for us, an oblation and a sacrifice to God for an odor of sweetness.

—*Eph. v, i, 2.*

THE GARDEN OF GETHSEMANI

When they had sung a hymn, they went forth to the Mount of Olives (Mark xiv, 26).

Then Jesus came with them into a country place which is called Gethsemani. And He said to His disciples: Sit you here till I go yonder and pray (Matt. xxvi, 36).

* * *

About a stone's throw from the Garden of Gethsemani was a grotto hewn out of the solid rock. The light was admitted into this grotto through a hole in the roof. In this country a custom prevailed of building cisterns for the purpose of holding rain-water. This fact, together with the form of the grotto and the aperture in the top, leads to the inference that it was formerly used as a cistern from which the garden was watered. At the time of our Lord it was old and abandoned, and no longer capable of retaining water, but it afforded the loiterer in the garden a place of refuge in warm or rainy weather. This grotto, now converted into a little chapel, still exists. It is called the Grotto of Agony, on account of the agony and bloody sweat which our Divine Saviour suffered there.

Having manifested to His three disciples the profound sadness under which He was laboring, Jesus said to them, "Sit ye here, till I go yonder and pray." The solitude of the place, the darkness of the night, the profound silence of nature, and the imminence of the hour of His capture—these were circumstances which combined to cause the Saviour to raise His voice in prayer to His Heavenly Father.

"Taking with Him Peter and the two sons of Zebedee, He began to grow sorrowful and to be sad."

"Then He saith to them: My soul is sorrowful even unto death. Stay you here and watch with Me."

"And going a little further, He fell upon His face, praying and saying: My Father, if it be possible, let this chalice pass from Me; nevertheless, not as I will but as Thou wilt" (Matt. xxvi, 37-39).

He Began to Grow Sorrowful

He began. This is what St. Augustine would call "a watchful word"; for there is a deep significance in it. Our Saviour has always had every detail of His passion before His mind; yet it is only now that He begins to show His sorrow. As for me, no sooner have I anything to suffer than I either grow fretful, or make a martyr of myself.

Let me learn to bear my sorrows in silence. *"Then He saith to them: My soul is sorrowful even unto death."* It would seem to have been God's purpose that His Son should die of a broken heart; but the malice of men has other tortures in store for Him: so He who gave men free will weaves their cruelty into His original design and suffers them to put their Saviour to death.

"Stay you here and watch with Me." Saying these words, He staggers forward under the great load of heart-rending sorrow, till He disappears from their sight in the little Grotto where He was wont to pray.

FEAR, SORROW, AND WEARINESS

The evangelists use three terms to describe what took place in our Saviour's soul: fear, sorrow, and weariness.

His fear arose from the anticipation of the awful tortures which were to come upon Him. He shrank from pain as we do, and was stricken with terror at the thought of the scourging and the nailing on the cross. "Father," He sobbed, "if it be possible, let this chalice pass from Me."

His sorrow was for the sins of men, my own sins among them, all of which were present to Him, all of which were laid upon Him as His own. And sin was not to Him what it is to us. Being God as well as man, He could measure its guilt, its degradation, its monstrous ingratitude, its fearful consequences; and it filled His soul with unutterable loathing, with heart-breaking grief.

His weariness was the result of unrequited love, the cruel sense of failure, the heartless waste of His blood, whereof so many for whom it was shed would make no use at all, would even turn it to their own damnation.

So intense was His anguish that first a cold sweat broke out all over His body standing in big drops upon His brow; then this sweat became tinged with blood, till at last it was pure blood that oozed from every pore, filling His garments and dropping from His face on to the ground.

Our Saviour's Prayer

"Father, if it be possible, let this chalice pass from Me." What an agony of woe breathes through this heart-broken petition! What fear, what sadness, what weariness! It teaches us that we, too, may pray for relief in sorrow; yet we must learn to add, as Jesus did: "Nevertheless not My will but Thine be done." His heart is perfectly submissive to the decree of His Father. While as man He recoils from the appalling sacrifice demanded of Him, His Father's will is His will; nor does He for one moment set Himself in opposition to it.

The Angel of Comfort

"And there appeared to Him an angel from heaven strengthening Him." This angel was sent to whisper to our Saviour's bleeding heart what that dark cloud of anguish had for the time obscured, the glory His Passion would give to God, the salvation of countless souls made in God's likeness, the repentance of sinners, the triumphs of His Church, the love of His saints, the generosity of His martyrs, the immaculate holiness of His Virgin Mother, all which were to be the fruit of the sufferings He was now to undergo. Stern comfort in truth; we in our weakness may think it cold comfort; yet Jesus was grateful to that blessed spirit and gathered new strength from His inspirations; nevertheless to the end of His prayer He went on repeating the same words. "My Father, if this chalice may not pass away, but I must drink it, Thy will be done" (Matt. xxvi, 42).

THE SLEEPING DISCIPLES

Angels cannot suffer and therefore, though full of pity, can not share in our sufferings; but Jesus is a real man and, like every son of Adam, feels the need of human sympathy; so, while the angel returns to heaven, He goes to look for His three chosen friends. He had told them to watch.

He now finds them sleeping. They have no sympathy to give Him; yet how gently He reproaches them! "Simon, sleepest thou? Couldst not thou watch with Me one hour? Watch and pray that ye enter not into temptation. The spirit indeed is willing; but the flesh is weak."

Our Saviour then returned to His solitary prayer, and when after a while He came back to them, "He found them again asleep, for their eyes were heavy; and they knew not what to answer Him." Am I not in just the same case? I have slept when I ought to have been watching; I have left my dear Lord to suffer alone, and I know not what to answer Him. All my grand protestations of love and loyalty have proved empty and worthless. I am, indeed, an unprofitable servant.

Christ has now entered into His eternal kingdom; yet He is still as human as ever. Has He not in these latter days come back to earth at Paray to complain that men love Him so little, to beg for their love? In the Holy Eucharist He is still longing for our sympathy.

It Might Have Been

"And He cometh the third time," His prayer being now finished, "and saith to them: Sleep on now and take your rest. Behold the hour is at hand, and the Son of man shall be betrayed into the hands of sinners." There is a gentle irony in these sad words which must have touched them to the quick. It is too late now; they have missed their opportunity; the hour is come and they are not ready for it.

What bitterness there is for all of us in the thought of what might have been! If I had been more faithful, if I had but watched and prayed, how far otherwise I should have borne myself under temptation! how much remorse I should have been spared! how much suffering I should have spared my Saviour!

Neither Peter, James, nor John had obeyed Our Lord's injunction; yet Peter fell terribly, James, like the rest, ran away. John was faithful to the end. How inscrutable are the ways of grace!

* * *

Today, if you shall hear His voice, harden not your hearts.
—*Ps. xciv, 8.*

The Lesson which we should learn from Christ's example in His agony is this—the necessity of prayer. But it is not sufficient to pray only in time of adversity; we should pray always, and pray with entire submission to the divine will. Let us expose to our dear Saviour all our wants and miseries; let us ask not only for salvation, but also for all the temporal blessings of which we may stand in need; let us ask Him for health and for preservation from all the accidents and dangers that surround our daily life. But let us ever make these requests in the spirit of the prayer of Jesus Christ, saying with Him, "Not as I will, but as Thou wilt."

* * *

This is the confidence which we have towards Him: That whatsoever we shall ask according to His will, He heareth us.
—*1 John v, 14.*

THE TRAITOR

"Judas having received a band of soldiers and servants from the chief Priests and the Pharisees, cometh thither with lanterns and torches and weapons.

Jesus therefore, knowing all things that should come upon Him, went forth and said to them: "Whom seek ye?" (John xviii, 5-4.)

With what serene majesty Our Saviour faces His foes! How calm and self-possessed! Like a brave captain in a storm at sea—nay, rather, like Himself as He stood up and quelled the winds and waves of Genesareth. "Whom seek ye?" "Jesus of Nazareth," say they. "I am He." No wonder "they went backward and fell to the ground;" for they seemed to hear the name of their God as Moses had received it ages ago: "I am Who am."

Our Lord had now declared Himself; so there was no further need for Judas to point Him out; but the poor wretch was afraid of losing his blood-money if he failed to fulfil his contract. It is hardly conceivable that he believed Jesus to be "the Son of the living God," as his fellow-apostles had done since Peter's confession. Perhaps his want of faith was one reason of his terrible abandonment; or he may have once had the faith and let it die out in his heart. That of course would explain everything.

So Judas now comes forward to fulfil his accursed bargain. "Friend," asks our Saviour, "whereto art thou come?" Was this said in irony? Oh, no! There was an awful irony, a most bitter jest in that "Hail, Rabbi!" of the traitor. He hails Christ as his Lord and Master at the very moment when he is giving himself for ever, body and soul, to Satan; but the good Jesus meant what He said. He called him friend because He longed to make him so. His heart was yearning for that perishing soul. Good Shepherd as He was, He was on the point of laying down His life for that lost sheep of His flock; but all is in vain. The cruel sign is given, and then, with a look of unutterable sadness Jesus says: "Judas, dost thou betray the Son of man with a kiss?" They were His last words to that false friend.

* * *

Among our Saviour's captors were "the chief priests and magistrates of the Temple and the ancients." These same men were present afterward at His crucifixion; yet, as they were His judges, their presence was not only unnecessary, but utterly unbecoming their position. Two things we gather from it:

1. Their intense malice against Our Lord.
2. That even before His trial they were resolved to convict Him.

This now brings upon them a severe reproof; for our Saviour throughout His passion, while saying nothing in His own defence, always speaks out fearlessly in the cause of justice. "Are you come out," He says, "as it were against a thief, with swords and clubs? When I was daily with you in the Temple you did not stretch forth your hands against Me; but this is your hour and the power of darkness." You are doing this, He adds, "that the Scriptures may be fulfilled."

Had not these wretched men quite silenced the voice of conscience this should have been enough to frighten them. They knew well what the prophets had said of the Messias, and what they were doing now and had it in their hearts to do was a literal fulfilment of those predictions. Yet when they had nailed Him on the cross they actually dared to quote against Him a psalm which they well knew to be Messianic: "He trusted God. Let Him now deliver Him, if He will have Him; for He said, I am the Son of God" (Ps. xxi, 9). O God! What a fearful thing it is to resist Thy grace! All this time they were strictly observing the law, fasting twice in the week, giving tithes of all that they possessed. What fearful self-deception!

* * *

Woe to you, scribes and Pharisees, hypocrites; because you make clean the outside of the cup and the dish, but within, you are full of rapine and uncleanness.

Thou blind Pharisee, first make clean the inside of the cup and of the dish, that the outside may become clean.

Woe to you, scribes and Pharisees, hypocrites; because you are like to whited sepulchres, which outwardly appear to men beautiful, but within, are full of dead men's bones, and of all filthiness.

So you also outwardly indeed appear to men just; but inwardly you are full of hypocrisy and iniquity.

—*Matt. xxiii, 25-28.*

Peter's Fall

The soldiers took Jesus and bound Him.

"And they led him away to Annas first, for he was the father-in-law to Caiphas, who was the high priest of that year.

"Now Caiphas was he who had given the counsel to the Jews: That it was expedient that one man should die for the people.

"And Simon Peter followed Jesus" (John xviii, 13-15).

Peter had followed our Lord *"afar off."* When he arrived at the court of the high priest he was refused admission; but John, recognizing his voice, spoke to the portress and brought in Peter. "The maid saith to Peter: Art thou not also one of this man's disciples? He saith: I am not."

This first denial was perhaps hardly deliberate. The question was unexpected and the reply sprung to his lips from a sudden instinct of self-preservation; but having made this first false step, he began to act a part, warming himself at the fire and joining in the talk around it, as though he were an indifferent spectator. He was now wholly under the influence of fear; for his one great object henceforth was to escape further notice.

O my God, give me grace to be on my guard against a first false move which may involve such fearful consequences; for if I do not take the first step I shall not take the second.

I Know Not This Man

Directly after this first denial the cock crew; but Peter did not notice it. Presently "another maid saw him, and she saith to them that were there: This man also was with Jesus of Nazareth. And again he denied, with an oath: I know not the man. And after a little while they that stood by came and said to Peter: Surely thou also art one of them; for even thy speech doth discover thee"— the Galileans apparently having a dialect of their own. "Then Peter began to curse and swear that he knew not the man; and immediately the cock crew again." That cock might have crowed himself hoarse before Peter heard him. Fear had now taken such complete possession of him that he was deaf to every warning.

How often has it been so with me! When under the dominion of some strong passion I reject all good advice and every holy inspiration. What would affect me deeply at another time has no power then. I am dragged along like a prisoner in chains.

Peter's Repentance

"And the Lord, turning, looked on Peter." It was a look full of sorrow and tender reproach. Not only Peter's cowardly denial, but countless others of which it was the type and sample were lying heavy on that loving heart. That look went straight to Peter's heart, recalling to his memory everything he had forgotten; his protestations of love and loyalty, the Lord's solemn but fruitless warnings, his neglect of prayer in the garden, all came back to him then, "and going forth he wept bitterly," or, as St. Mark puts it so tenderly: "he began to weep." Yes, Peter began to weep, and till his dying day, we are told, he could never hear the cock crow but his grief broke forth anew, till that worn face of his was furrowed with the tears that were always falling.

If I have sinned like Peter, God grant me grace to repent like Peter.

* * *

A sacrifice to God is an afflicted spirit: a contrite and humbled heart, O God, thou wilt not despise.
—Ps. l, 19.

* * *

Thou hast mercy upon all, because Thou canst do all things, and overlookest the sins of men for the sake of repentance.
—Wis. xi, 24.

Jesus Before Caiphas the High Priest

The chief priests and the whole council sought false witness against Jesus, that they might put Him to death (Matt. xxvi).

They themselves were His judges; but, being already resolved on His death, they stooped to the basest means to accomplish their purpose. Mark how jealousy and hatred degrade the character and darken the conscience.

"Their evidence did not agree." Alas! there is no need to bring forsworn witnesses against me. How many there are who can bear true evidence, my own conscience confirming all they say! I will plead guilty, therefore, and throw myself on God's great mercy, that I may not be convicted and condemned at the last day.

"And the high priests, rising up, said to Him: Answerest Thou nothing to the things which these witness against Thee? But Jesus held His peace." Another lesson for me. Have I ever held my peace under a false accusation? Why, it is as much as I can do to be silent under a true one. "And the high priest said to Him: I adjure Thee by the living God that Thou tell us if Thou be the Christ, the Son of God." Then out of reverence for the office Caiphas held and still more for His Father's name Jesus replied: "I am. Nevertheless, I say to you, hereafter you shall see the Son of man sitting on the right hand of the power of God, and coming in the clouds of heaven."

The Son of man, who is also the Son of God, shall come to judge the world, and then shall these very men who are now about to condemn Him to death be brought before Him for condemnation.

JESUS IS CONDEMNED

"Then the high priest, rending his garments, saith: What need we any further witnesses? You have heard the blasphemy; what think you? And they all condemned Him to be guilty of death." Thus by a formal act of the great council of His chosen people the God of Israel was finally and forever rejected.

As Our Lord stood there before them He thought of all that He had done for them in their long history of two thousand years; how He had brought them out of the land of Egypt in signs and wonders; how patiently He had borne with their idolatries; how often He had warned and threatened them; how mercifully He had chastized and forgiven them. He thought of his own preaching through their cities and villages, of the miracles He had wrought to convert them and induce them to accept Him as their promised Redeemer. All has been in vain. They have cast Him off. "He came unto His own, and His own received Him not" (John i, 11). And this great crime, like every other throughout the passion, was to Christ a typical one, a sample of what was to be repeated again and again. Individual men and whole nations, too, would renounce their allegiance to Him, revolt against His Church and break away into heresy and schism. Oh, let me once more vow fealty to my Saviour and by my devotion atone for the disloyalty He meets with on every side.

* * *

God is faithful: by whom you are called unto the fellowship of His Son, Jesus Christ our Lord.

—*1 Cor. i, 9.*

* * *

May the God of peace Himself sanctify you in all things; that your whole spirit, and soul, and body, may be preserved blameless in the coming of our Lord Jesus Christ.
—*1 Thess. v, 23, 24.*

Jesus Is Mocked and Blindfolded. He Is Left All Night in the Hands of His Guards

The Council broke up, everyone going to his home, while Jesus was left to be the sport of the servants. "Then did they spit in His face and buffet Him. And others struck His face with the palms of their hands." Jesus was silent under these gross insults.

As for me, I can not bear the smallest insult. A blow in the face would make me furious; but to be spat upon! Oh, I could not tolerate that! Yet see how patiently Christ endures it all. "They blindfolded Him and smote Him on the face, saying: Prophesy unto us, O Christ, who is he that struck Thee?"

This is all we know of the events of that night. What a night it must have been for Jesus, all alone among these savages! The unrecorded sufferings of our Saviour should teach us the priceless value of those sorrows which, borne in silence and hidden from men, are known only to God.

St. John now goes to visit our blessed Lady and to tell her all that has taken place. So while Jesus spends a sleepless night in the hands of His torturers Mary is watching and weeping in sympathy with her Son. It would be a hard heart that did not feel for them.

Hear, O ye heavens, and give ear, O earth, for the Lord hath spoken. I have brought up children, and exalted them: but they have despised me.

The ox knoweth his owner, and the ass his master's crib: but Israel hath not known Me, and My people hath not understood.

Woe to the sinful nation, a people laden with iniquity, ungracious children: they have forsaken the Lord, they have blasphemed the Holy One of Israel, they are gone away backwards.

—Is. i, 2-4.

* * *

My heart hath expected reproach and misery.

And I looked for one that would grieve together with Me, but there was none: and for one that would comfort Me, and I found none.

—Ps. ixviii, 21.

CHRIST BEFORE PILATE

The sun had already risen, and was spreading its beneficent rays far and wide over the plains of Judea, when, the sentence of death having been definitively pronounced, Jesus was again loaded with chains and dragged to the palace of Pontius Pilate.

Pilate was the Roman governor of Judea, to whom alone belonged the power, not only to execute the sentence of death, but also to judge whether those brought before his tribunal were deserving of such sentence.

Arriving at the gate of Pilate's palace, the chief priests and ancients halted, because this being the place where criminals were condemned, these hypocrites feared that by entering they should contaminate themselves and become irregular and unclean and consequently unfit to offer sacrifice or participate in the solemnities of the approaching feast of the Pasch. So they delivered Jesus to the guards with orders to bring Him before Pilate and to request that official, in their name and that of the Jewish people, to deign to expedite the trial by ratifying at once the sentence of death already pronounced. They added that the affair was one of urgent importance, and for this reason they themselves had come to the palace, though, acting in compliance with their own law, they dared not enter its portals.

Our Lord's accusers, being scrupulous observers of the law, "went not into the hall, that they might not be defiled"; yet they are quite ready to shed innocent blood. Have I never been a whited sepulchre, never strained out a gnat and swallowed a camel? When Pilate asks: "What accusation bring you against this man?" they show no hesitation in altering the charge, so as to influence the governor's mind against Him. Christ had been condemned because He declared Himself the Son of God. The charges they now allege are totally different: "We have found this man perverting our nation and forbidding to give tribute to Caesar and saying that he is Christ the King."

These charges we know were utterly false. Our Lord had not perverted the people. As to the tribute, He had said: "Give unto Caesar the things that are Caesar's." He had hidden Himself when the people would have made Him king. But their object now is to represent Him as a rebel against the authority of their hated conquerors, the Romans.

"Answerest Thou nothing? said Pilate. Behold in how many things they accuse Thee. But Jesus still answered nothing, so that Pilate wondered." He had not come to defend Himself; He had only come to die.

Hail, King of the Jews

The governor then examined Our Lord privately. "Art Thou the King of the Jews? he asked. Jesus answered: Thou sayest (truly) that I am a king. But My kingdom is not of this world. If My kingdom were of this world, My servants would certainly strive that I should not be delivered to the Jews: but now My kingdom is not from hence."

The Gospel narrative goes on as follows:

"When He was accused by the chief priests and ancients, He answered nothing.

"Then Pilate saith to Him: Dost not Thou hear how great testimonies they allege against Thee?

"And He answered him to never a word, so that the governor wondered exceedingly.

"Now upon the solemn day the governor was accustomed to release to the people one prisoner, whom they would.

"And he had then a notorious prisoner that was called Barabbas.

"They therefore being gathered together, Pilate said: Whom will you that I release to you: Barabbas, or Jesus that is called Christ?

"For he knew that for envy they had delivered Him.

"And as he was sitting in the place of judgment, his wife sent to him, saying: Have thou nothing to do with that just man; for I have suffered many things this day in a dream because of Him.

"But the chief priests and ancients persuaded the people that they should ask Barabbas and make Jesus away.

"And the governor answering, said to them: Whether will you of the two to be released unto you? But they said: Barabbas.

"Pilate saith to them: What shall I do then with Jesus that is called Christ? They say all: Let Him be crucified.

"The governor said to them: Why, what evil hath He done? But they cried out the more, saying: Let Him be crucified.

"And Pilate seeing that he prevailed nothing, but that rather a tumult was made, taking water washed his hands before the people, saying: I am innocent of the blood of this just man. Look you to it.

"And the whole people answering, said: His blood be upon us and upon our children.

"Then he released to them Barabbas: and having scourged Jesus, delivered Him unto them to be crucified.

"Then the soldiers of the governor, taking Jesus into the hall, gathered together unto Him the whole band.

"And stripping Him, they put a scarlet cloak about Him.

"And platting a crown of thorns, they put it upon His head, and a reed in His right hand. And bowing the knee before Him, they mocked Him, saying: Hail, King of the Jews.

"And spitting upon Him, they took the reed and struck His head.

"And after they had mocked Him, they took off the cloak from Him and put on Him His own garments and led Him away to crucify Him" (Matt. xxvii, 12-31).

Crucify Him

The sin-soaked earth is thirsting for the blood of a Redeemer.

Crucify Him because Cain hated Abel, because of the wickedness that brought about the Flood, because of the nameless abomination of the cities of the plain, because of the idolatries, and harlotries of the chosen people. Crucify Him because of the pride of the pharisee, the hollow-heartedness of the scribe, the filthiness of Herod's court, the cowardly injustice of Pilate. Crucify Him for the sins of Christian nations, for the sins of my own people, for my sins, O God, for my sins!

Pilate gave orders that Jesus should be scourged. That was the usual preliminary to crucifixion; yet Pilate still hoped that it might satisfy the people. "I will scourge Him," he had said, "and let Him go." How often have I said the same! How often have I flattered myself that I could gratify some sinful inclination to a certain point, and then stop! But one sin has led to another, till, like Pilate, I have first scourged my Saviour and then crucified Him.

* * *

And the Eternal Wisdom is treated as a fool. Shall I not bear a little shame, then, for His sake?

"If any man among you seem to be wise in this world let him become as a fool, that he may be wise; for the wisdom of this world is foolishness with God" (1 Cor. iii, 18).

* * *

Love not the world, nor the things which are in the world. If any man love the world, the charity of the Father is not in him.

For all that is in the world, is the concupiscence of the flesh, and the concupiscence of the eyes, and the pride of life, which is not of the Father, but is of the world.

And the world passeth away, and the concupiscence thereof: but he that doth the will of God, abideth for ever.
—1 John ii, 15-17.

* * *

THE DREADFUL TORMENT AT THE PILLAR

The passion of Jesus Christ was most bitter in all its stages, but the excess of that bitterness can be realized only by those who meditate profoundly on its particular incidents, among which there are few more touching than that of the scourging at the pillar. Nevertheless, the Evangelists pass over in silence all the impious circumstances connected with it, and the barbarity of the manner of its execution, and content themselves with saying that

Pilate, seeing that he could not convince the Jews of Jesus' innocence, caused Him to be scourged, hoping that this cruel spectacle might, perhaps, move them to compassion. "Then therefore Pilate took Jesus, and scourged Him."

The Evangelists also relate the crowning of our Saviour with thorns, and the crucifixion, two most painful events in the passion, with the same simplicity and conciseness, leaving it to the piety of the Christian to realize the atrocity of the Saviour's sufferings.

There was an atrium, or court-yard, at the entrance of Pilate's tribunal, and in this court-yard stood a marble column, rising only a few spans above the ground. A criminal condemned to be scourged was bound to this column by means of ropes passed around the lower portion of the body, his hands were tied behind his back, and more than half his person was exposed to the lash.

Scourging was an infamous torture inflicted only on slaves condemned to capital punishment, and was considered so atrocious that the Jews, a civilized people, or at least a people less barbarous than their contemporaries, in the infliction of this punishment were limited by law to thirty-nine lashes. Among the Romans, a cruel and sanguinary people, there was no limit assigned, but the number of lashes to be inflicted was regulated by the cruelty or humanity of the judge, and sometimes the matter was left entirely to the discretion of the executioner.

Jesus, therefore, having been condemned to be scourged, was dragged by the executioners to the court-yard of the tribunal, where a great crowd had assembled to witness the inhuman spectacle. Arrived on the ground, Jesus divested Himself of His robes, and then without any compulsion—as was revealed to St. Bridget—He presented His hands to the executioners, to have them tied, and offered Himself to be fastened to the pillar.

A certain number of men are told off to scourge Him in relays. We see them throwing off their tunics, turning up their sleeves and each choosing out his whip or bundle of rods, as if they were making ready for a game. It is mere sport to them, and they laugh and jest as they make their preparations.

Now they fall to. The rods come first, stripping the skin away; then the whips, loaded with lead or iron, till every part of that sacred body is crushed and mangled and the very bones laid bare, each well-aimed blow being applauded by the savage bystanders. At length they are all weary and the torture ceases; the rope is cut, and Jesus falls senseless to the ground. Then maybe they throw cold water on His face to bring Him to. He rises painfully, trembling in every limb, and is left to put on His garments as best He may.

This fearful torment was the penalty for my sins of impurity. Every sensual action, every carnal desire was present to my dear Lord as He groaned under those merciless scourges. Can I ever dare to commit such sins again? Do I not grieve over them now? Am I not eager to take vengeance on this flesh, which through its selfish greed for pleasure has brought such cruel suffering on my Redeemer?

* * *

With all watchfulness keep thy heart, because life issueth out from it.
—*Prov. iv, 23.*

* * *

He that loveth cleanness of heart, for the grace of his lips, shall have the king for his friend.
—*Prov. xxii, 11.*

* * *

Blessed are the clean of heart: for they shall see God.
—*Matt. v, 8.*

* * *

And we know that to them that love God, all things work together unto good, to such as, according to His purpose, are called to be saints.
—*Rom. viii, 28.*

Grace be with all them that love our Lord Jesus Christ in incorruption. Amen.
—*Eph. vi, 24.*

The Crowning With Thorns

Quivering from that cruel scourging, Our Saviour sits crouched up on a stool set against the wall. The soldiers say: "He calls Himself a king, does He? Then we will give Him kingly honors." We are told that the whole cohort was gathered together for this sport. Now the full tale of a Roman cohort was 600 men; and, though some of this force may have been on duty in other parts of the city, we may be sure Pilate kept a strong body of soldiers about his person during the anxious days of the festival. A hundred men, then, at the least must have spat in Our Lord's face that day, after they had placed upon His head the cruel crown of thorns.

We see them falling in, two and two, in mock procession, laughing and jesting noisily the while, each couple in turn bending the knee before Him, striking His head with the reed and hawking up all the filth in their lungs to spit it in His blessed face. What a sight He must have been when that sport was over! Great God in heaven! this is Thy beloved Son in whom Thou art well pleased; how then canst Thou look down upon this scene and not destroy the world which thus illtreats Him?

This is the atonement my Saviour offers for my pride. I hold my head so high; I stand so much on my dignity; I am so impatient under the smallest slight or insult; so my Lord must be humbled to the dust, mocked, and flouted, and spat upon. Oh, surely I will begin now to wage war upon this accursed pride of mine, to humble myself, and to welcome humiliation for love of my despised Redeemer.

* * *

Never suffer pride to reign in thy mind, or in thy words; for from it all perdition took its beginning.

Job. iv, 14.

THE MEETING OF JESUS AND MARY

At this moment He sees His blessed Mother trying to approach Him. Their eyes just meet and then she is pushed rudely aside and the soldiers hurry Him along.

Poor broken-hearted Mother! Years ago it had been a rapturous happiness to look forward to His birth; but it was a deeper joy still to see Him lying on her breast, to press her lips to His. So now, though it has been agony untold to look forward to His passion, it is far more terrible than she ever thought it would be. Many a time has she tried to picture this scene to herself; but she never imagined her Jesus would look like this, torn, crushed, and beaten almost out of recognition even by her, His own Mother. Thus is the anguish of a lifetime's fearful anticipation concentrated in a single look.

SIMON OF CYRENE HELPS JESUS TO CARRY HIS CROSS

It is now quite evident that unless He is dealt with more gently, Our Saviour will die upon the way, and that is not at all the intention of His enemies. Just at this moment Simon of Cyrene, coming in from the country, meets the crowd surging out of the city, and, catching sight of his beloved Master—for everything tends to show that he was a disciple—is moved, like the Good Samaritan, with compassion. The high priests mark his sympathy for their victim and that is enough for them. "Make this man help Him," they cry. So Simon is forced to carry the cross "after Jesus;" that is to say, they carry it between them. Our Lady sees what is done and blesses Simon from her heart. Who would not wish to share in Mary's blessing? Who would not gladly help Jesus to carry His cross?

Unto you it is given for Christ, not only to believe in Him, but also to suffer for Him.

—Philipp. i, 29.

* * *

In all things we suffer tribulation, but are not distressed; we are straitened, but are not destitute;

We suffer persecution, but are not forsaken; we are cast down, but we perish not;

Always bearing about in our body the mortification of Jesus, that the life also of Jesus may be made manifest in our bodies.

—2 Cor. iv, 8-10.

* * *

And all that will live godly in Christ Jesus, shall suffer persecution.

—2 Tim. iii, 12.

Veronica Wipes Our Lord's Face

Women throughout the Passion come to the front, showing without fear their sympathy for Our Saviour. Tradition has preserved a touching incident that now befell. A lady of Jesusalem, named Veronica, seeing Our Lord's exhaustion and His face covered with filth and blood, comes forward to offer Him a handkerchief. Jesus accepts it and, having wiped His face, returns it to her with the impress of His sacred countenance upon it. Our Lady sees this also, and how she blesses the loving devotion of Veronica! She blesses every one who does anything for Jesus. Shortly after this Our Lord falls again. At length Our Saviour arrives at the foot of Calvary where He falls a third time; but they drag Him up the slope—a short ascent, yet how painful? I have often toiled up a much higher hill than this in the hope of seeing a fine view from its summit; but the only prospect before Jesus Christ is the nailing of His hands and feet and the three hours' agony.

At last the top is reached, and the executioners fall to work at once; for there is no time to lose. All must be over by sundown, the bodies must be taken away and buried, and the divine victim is eager too; "What thou dost, do quickly."

* * *

Behold, I come quickly, and My reward is with Me, to render to every man according to his works.

—*Apoc. xxii, 12.*

* * *

Now all chastisement for the present indeed seemeth not to bring with it joy, but sorrow: but afterwards it will yield, to them that are exercised by it, the most peaceable fruit of justice.

—*Heb. xxi, 11.*

JESUS NAILED TO THE CROSS

While the two beams of the cross are being fastened together Our Saviour is offered wine mingled with gall or myrrh, "which when He had tasted He would not drink"; for the effect would have been to stupefy as well as to strengthen Him.

After this He is stripped of His clothes, which have now become glued to His wounds, so that the pain is very great, and no attempt is made to lessen it. Then lying down on the cross He stretches forth His hands to be nailed. The crowd presses round, those behind craning their necks to see over the shoulders of those in front. The thieves attract less attention; for they are but common criminals, and they are only to be bound to their gibbets, whereas Christ is to be nailed, and the cruel sport is always the popular one.

A huge nail is now placed on the palm of the right hand and with one swinging blow is driven through it into the wood; then stroke follows stroke, sending it well home. Then the left hand and then the feet are fastened in like manner.[1]

---

[1] The above is the traditional conception of Our Lord's crucifixion. The ordinary process, however, was first to nail the hands on the crossbeam and then to haul the body up with ropes till it rested on a crutch or saddle fixed on the upright post. The crossbeam was then fastened in position and the feet were drawn together and nailed.

Mary At the Foot of the Cross

The blessed Mother is standing at the foot of the little hill, unable to get nearer by reason of the crowd. She does not hear the first blow; but the second, third, and fourth she hears as they drive the nails home into the hard wood, carrying the skin and flesh of her Son with them. Ah, think what each stroke of the hammer meant to her! Now amid shouts of delight and derision the cross is raised, her beloved impaled upon it. She watches—poor Mother—as its foot is dragged along the rough ground and then dropped suddenly into the deep hole dug for it, and anon comes the driving in of stakes to steady it, every jolt and blow causing new agony to the patient Victim.

* * *

Now the centurion and his men force the crowd back, and slowly, with the help of John and Magdalen, she moves up through that dense throng to take her appointed place beneath the gibbet of her Son.

O most afflicted Mother! to what shall I compare thee, or to what shall I liken thee, O Daughter of Jerusalem, in order to form even a faint idea of thy immense grief? Alas! only the depths of the sea can give me any conception of the depths of thy grief!

The Evangelists relate that, immediately after the crucifixion, four of the soldiers who had taken an active part in the execution of the unjust sentence gathered together the garments of Jesus, and dividing them into four parts, took each a part. But for the seamless tunic which His Mother had made they cast lots, not wishing to spoil it by dividing it.

While this division was being made the people passed and repassed under the cross, insulting Jesus, wagging their heads in mockery, and vomiting forth against Him the most horrible blasphemies. This was not done by the rabble alone, but also by the chief priests, the scribes and Pharisees. All these things had been foretold by the prophet, who, speaking in the person of the suffering Saviour, said: "All they that saw Me have laughed Me to scorn: they have spoken with the lips, and wagged the head. And I am become a reproach to them: they saw Me, and they shook their heads" (Psalms xxi, 8; cviii, 25). Some cried out to Him, "If Thou be the Son of God, come down from the cross, and we will believe in Thee." Others said, "He saved others; Himself He cannot save. Vah, Thou that destroyest the temple of God and in three days dost rebuild it: save Thy own self." Others again said, with bitter irony, "He hoped in the Lord, let the Lord deliver Him: let Him save Him, seeing He delighteth in Him. For if He be the true Son of God, He will defend Him, and will deliver Him from the hands of His enemies." But what does Jesus answer to all these insults and blasphemies? Raising His languid eyes towards heaven, He prays, "Father, forgive them, for they know not what they do."

* * *

And they shall say to Him: What are these wounds in the midst of Thy hands? And He shall say: With these I was wounded in the house of them that loved Me.

—*Zach. xiv, 6.*

* * *

They have pierced My hands and My feet; they have numbered all my bones.

—*Ps. xxi, 17, 18.*

THE TITLE OF THE CROSS

Pilate wrote a title also, and he put it upon the cross: and the writing was: *"Jesus of Nazareth, the King of the Jews."*

Jesus:—This holy name means Saviour. It was decreed for Him before His birth: "Thou shalt call His name Jesus; for He shall save His people from their sins" (Matt. i, 21). It was solemnly given to Him at His circumcision, when His precious blood was first shed. Now He is pouring forth that blood to the last drop; the work of Redemption will soon be complete. It is a glorious name. "He humbled Himself, becoming obedient unto death, even to the death of the cross. For which cause God also hath exalted Him, and hath given Him a name which is above all names; that in the name of Jesus every knee should bow, of those that are in heaven, on earth, and under the earth; and that every tongue should confess that the Lord Jesus Christ is in the glory of God the Father" (Philipp. ii, 8).

Of Nazareth:—This reminds us of the life of humble toil now ending in such a cruel and shameful death. He has been poor and in labors from His youth. He has lived only to do the will of His Father, and He does it to the end.

King:—1. By inheritance, as the Son of His eternal Father: "I am appointed king by Him over Sion, His holy mountain" (Ps. ii, 6).

2. By nature, having all the qualities of a king—wisdom, justice, power, mercy, a royal mind and heart. He is every inch a king.

3. By conquest:—"Gird Thy sword upon Thy thigh, O Thou most mighty. With Thy comeliness and Thy beauty, set out, proceed prosperously, and reign" (Ps. xliv, 4, 5). "The Lord said to my Lord: Sit Thou at My right hand till I make Thy enemies Thy footstool" (Ps. cix, 1).

Of the Jews:—The very title the Magi had given Him at His birth: "Where is He that is born King of the Jews?" But the Jews would not have Him. "We will not have this man to reign over us" (Luke xix, 14). "He came unto His own and His own received Him not. But as many as received Him He gave them power to be made the sons of God, to them that believe in His name" (John i, 11, 12).

Our Lord's Kingdom Is Not of This World

Our Lord's kingdom is "not of this world"; yet He is to reign over the hearts of men to the end of time, and so the inscription "was written in Hebrew, in Greek, and in Latin," to show forth His universal dominion over the souls His blood has redeemed.

And I have sworn fealty to Him, again and again, declaring Him my king and my God. If I have proved unfaithful and disloyal, let me now return to my allegiance, and serve Him henceforth with all my heart, all my mind, and all my strength.

What I Have Written I Have Written

"The chief priests of the Jews said to Pilate: Write not the King of the Jews, but that He said I am the King of the Jews. Pilate answered: What I have written I have written."

Here Pilate shows a firmness we should not have expected of him. He has yielded on every other point; he will not yield on this; but his firmness is not his own. It is the Holy Spirit that forbids him to make any changes. These words are to remain forever in condemnation of the Jews and of all who, like them, refuse to acknowledge the King of Kings.

* * *

I will extol Thee, O God my King, and I will bless Thy name for ever: yea, for ever and ever.

—Ps. cxliv, 1.

* * *

To the King of ages, immortal, invisible, the only God, be honor and glory for ever and ever.

—1 Tim. 17.

* * *

Thy kingdom!

—Matt. vi, 10.

THE FIRST WORD FROM THE CROSS

Jesus said: "Father, forgive them; for they know not what they do."

The Divine Master distinctly taught His disciples to pray: "Forgive us our trespasses as we forgive them that trespass against us." And He has told us that we must forgive, not seven times only, but seventy times seven, that with what measure we mete it shall be measured to us again. It is a hard lesson for corrupt human nature to learn, so He makes it easier for us by His example—by His own beautiful forgiveness.

FORGIVE THEM: FOR THEY KNOW NOT WHAT THEY DO

Oh, the marvel of it! Do they not know? The Roman soldiers, of course, know not; how can they?

But the Jewish people, their leaders above all—surely they can not be excused. In truth they know enough to make them terribly guilty; yet they know not as they might know, as they will know some day. And so He finds excuse even for them, pleads for them all, offering His blood in atonement for their sin, like the Good Shepherd that He is. "He hath borne the sins of many, and hath prayed for the transgressors" (Is. liii, 12).

I also was included in that prayer; yet how could He find excuse for me? I am a Christian. I have received so many sacraments, such a wealth of grace. I know so much more than they who brought about His death. Yes, I know indeed, and yet I know not. When I stand before Him for judgment, then at last I shall understand what sin means. So my good Jesus pleads for me: "He knows not what he does."

And He would have me forgive even as He has forgiven me. Have I got this lesson into my heart? Shall I ever master it? Yet how dare I say the "Our Father" unless I forgive? Is it not to call down God's vengeance on myself?

* * *

Then came Peter unto Him, and said: "Lord, how often shall my brother offend against me, and I forgive him? till seven times?"

Jesus saith to him: "I say not to thee till seven times; but till seventy times seven times."

—*Matt. xviii, 21, 22.*

* * *

And when you shall stand to pray, forgive, if you have aught against any man; that your Father also who is in heaven, may forgive you your sins.

But if you will not forgive, neither will your Father that is in heaven, forgive you your sins.

—*Mark xi, 25, 26.*

* * *

Judge not, and you shall not be judged. Condemn not, and you shall not be condemned. Forgive, and you shall be forgiven.
—*Luke vi, 37.*

THE SECOND WORD FROM THE CROSS

The dying Saviour said to the penitent thief: "Amen, I say to thee, this day shalt thou be with Me in Paradise."

Everyone about the cross is blaspheming and reviling, and the two thieves from their crosses join in. Hardened ruffians they, dying impenitent deaths. What should they know about Jesus of Nazareth? All the world says He is an impostor, so of course it must be true. He calls Himself the Christ, the Son of God; a merry jest to be sure; so in the midst of their own agony they laugh at Him. "If Thou art Christ save Thyself and us." But presently one of them catches that marvelous prayer of forgiveness. "Great God, instead of cursing His tormentors, as we do, He is asking pardon for them! Impossible, unless He is what He claims to be. Of a truth it must be the promised Messias;" so the scoffer stops his ribaldry and listens. Again the same words. Then in quick succession, as faith enters his soul, he strives to silence his fellow, confesses his own guilt, and proclaims the innocence of Christ.

Grace has been offered and accepted, and now it comes back in full flood, bringing complete faith with it. This man dying beside him is his King, his God. One mass of wounds, as he sees Him, He is on the point of entering into His kingdom. Upon no earthly throne will He ever sit. His kingdom is not of this world but of heaven. "Lord, remember me when Thou comest into Thy kingdom," he prays.

And Jesus said to him: "Amen, I say to thee, this day shalt thou be with Me in paradise."

This dying criminal is conscious of a long life of sin: he does not dream that he can enter at once into God's kingdom; all he craves is to be remembered in his place of exile. And Christ's reply grants much more than is asked; not only will He remember His fellow-sufferer, but in reward of his great faith and contrition bring him this very day into paradise. His cruel death in union with that of his Saviour shall be taken in full atonement for the shameful past.

On Calvary we learn that suffering is the law under which we all have to live, a law no child of Adam can hope to evade; for here we see three crucified together, the innocent, the hardened sinner, the humble penitent. Suffering, therefore, being unavoidable, we should try to get some good out of it, and when borne for Christ and with Christ how rich in blessings it is! With what giant strides we can tread the ways of holiness when we are nailed upon the cross with Christ!

* * *

With Christ I am nailed to the cross.

—Gal. ii, 19.

* * *

But God forbid that I should glory, save in the cross of our Lord Jesus Christ; by whom the world is crucified to me, and I to the world.

—Gal. vi, 14.

THE THIRD WORD FROM THE CROSS

"When Jesus therefore had seen His Mother and the disciple standing whom He loved. He saith to His Mother: Woman, behold thy son. After that He saith to the disciple: Behold thy Mother. And from that hour the disciple took her to his own."

From the poor criminal steeped till this moment in iniquity Our Saviour turns to His sinless Mother. She is standing now close to Him and John, the beloved disciple of Our Lord, at the other side.

"Woman," He says. Ah, what a beautiful name to those who believe in the Incarnation! What name can become her so well? It is her prophetic name, her official title: "I will put enmity between thee and the woman." It is this name that gives her her right to be here, *the second Eve* by the side of *the second Adam*.

"Behold thy son! Behold thy Mother!"

John stands there for all of us; and what a gift is this last bequest of the Sacred Heart! We might have thought He had nothing further to give.

"What is there that I ought to do more to My vineyard that I have not done to it?" (Is. v, 4).

Yet there is one gift left, and He knows well the value of it. It is the dearest treasure He possesses, dearer to Him than His own heart's blood. "*Behold thy Mother!* What she has been to Me, that she shall be to each one of you. Be you her children, and she, the Mother of your God, shall be a mother to you."

"And from that hour the disciple took her to his own." I, too, will take her to my own, loving her for her own sake and for His who died for me. She gave Him to me. She became His Mother to redeem me from death and hell. The precious blood He shed for me once ran in her pure veins and gushed from her virgin heart. O Mother of my God made man, be thou my mother and I will always be thy loving and devoted child.

* * *

Salve Regina

Hail, holy Queen, Mother of mercy, hail, our life, our sweetness, and our hope! To thee do we cry, poor banished children of Eve, to Thee do we send up our sighs, mourning and weeping in this valley of tears. Turn, then, most gracious advocate, thine eyes of mercy toward us; and after this our exile show unto us the blessed fruit of thy womb, Jesus, O clement, O loving, O sweet Virgin Mary.

* * *

Now the generation of Christ was in this wise. When His Mother Mary was espoused to Joseph, before they came together, she was found with child, of the Holy Ghost.

Whereupon Joseph her husband, being a just man and not willing publicly to expose her, was minded to put her away privately.

But while he thought on these things, behold the angel of the Lord appeared to him in his sleep, saying: Joseph, son of David, fear not to take unto thee Mary thy wife, for that which is conceived in her, is of the Holy Ghost.

And she shall bring forth a son: and thou shalt call his name Jesus. For He shall save His people from their sins.

Now all this was done that it might be fulfilled which the Lord spoke by the prophet, saying:

Behold a Virgin shall be with child and bring forth a man: and they shall call His name Emmanuel, which being interpreted is, God with us.

And Joseph rising up from sleep did as the angel of the Lord had commanded him and took unto him his wife.
—*Matt. i, 18, 24.*

THE FOURTH WORD FROM THE CROSS

"And about the ninth hour Jesus cried with a loud voice, saying: Eli, Eli, lamma sabacthani; My God, My God, why hast Thou forsaken Me?"

From the moment of the crucifixion a preternatural gloom had begun to gather over the sky, growing deeper and deeper as the hours wore on, and chilling every heart with awe and foreboding. The crowd dispersed. Many went home striking their breasts, conscious now that a great crime had been committed. A few of Our Lord's most savage persecutors remained to see the end and to taunt Him even in the moment of death. The centurion and his soldiers were still on duty, and Our Lady, John, and the little band of devoted women were gathered about their dying Saviour, the silence being broken only by the sobs of Magdalen and her fellow mourners.

Meantime the Heart of Christ is breaking with unutterable sorrow. His bodily tortures have hitherto veiled the anguish of His soul; but it has gone on all the while as we saw it in Gethsemani. He no longer sweats blood, for His blood has free passage now by a thousand open wounds and is nearly exhausted; but the same heavy load of weariness and grief is weighing on His heart, the sins of men, their cruel ingratitude and indifference, the waste of His precious blood through the loss of countless souls for whom He has shed it so unstintingly. It was decreed that the chalice should not pass away and so He is drinking it to the dregs. His soul is sorrowful even unto death; He has gone down into utter darkness.

"My God, My God," He cries, "why hast Thou forsaken Me?" (Ps. xxi, 2). To His heavenly Father He is always unspeakably dear; there can be no real separation between them; yet, in some way we cannot understand, for He always enjoyed the Beatific Vision, from His human soul the light of God's countenance is now hidden by a dense cloud of sadness. His cry comes out of the depths, and His Father seems not to hear.

Why should our dear Lord endure this terrible abandonment? That at my last hour God may not abandon me. The darkness of Christ's soul is the light of mine; His desolation is my eternal hope.

* * *

Blessed are those servants, whom the Lord when He cometh, shall find watching. Amen, I say to you, that He will gird Himself, and make them sit down to meat and passing will minister unto them.

—*Luke xii, 37.*

* * *

Watch ye, therefore, praying at all times, that you may be accounted worthy to escape all these things that are to come, and to stand before the Son of man.

—*Luke xxi, 36.*

* * *

For yourselves know perfectly, that the day of the Lord shall so come, as a thief in the night. . . .

But you, brethren, are not in darkness, that that day should overtake you as a thief.

For all you are the children of light, and children of the day: we are not of the night, nor of darkness.

Therefore, let us not sleep, as others do; but let us watch, and be sober.
—1 Thess. v, 2, 4-6.

* * *

Let us hold fast the confession of our hope without wavering (for He is faithful that hath promised).

And let us consider one another, to provoke unto charity and to good works:

Not forsaking our assembly, as some are accustomed: but comforting one another, and so much the more as you see the day approaching.
—Heb. x, 23-25.

* * *

The end of all is at hand. Be prudent, therefore, and watch in prayers.
—1 Peter iv, 7.

THE FIFTH WORD FROM THE CROSS

Jesus, knowing that all things were now accomplished, that the Scripture might be fulfilled, said: "I thirst."

A soldier hearing Christ say: "I thirst," came up with a sponge filled with vinegar, the acid wine provided for the soldiers, which he had set upon a reed, that he might moisten the parched lips of our dying Saviour. This, we may well believe, was kindly meant. It was the only act of consideration shown to Our Lord by his executioners and was no doubt richly rewarded. But the Jews cried out: "Let be! let us see whether Elias will come to deliver Him."

They pretended that the cry: "Eli, Eli;" "My God, My God," was meant for "Elias." "This man," they said, "called Elias."

Nevertheless the soldier reached up the sponge and pressed it against Our Lord's mouth. "In My thirst," sang the Psalmist, "they gave me vinegar to drink" (Ps. lxviii, 22).

Our Saviour's thirst must have been terrible indeed. Nothing had passed His lips since He left the supper chamber the evening before; for, though He had tasted the soothing potion offered to Him before His crucifixion, "He would not drink"; and now for more than twelve hours He has been suffering and bleeding continuously. "My strength is dried up like a potsherd and my tongue hath cleaved to my jaws and Thou hast brought me down into the dust of death" (Ps. xxi, 16).

Fearful as was Our Lord's bodily thirst, that of His soul was far harder to bear. As the hart pants after the waterbrooks, so did He long for the love of men; yet how often was this to be denied Him! How many would give Him the vinegar of ingratitude instead of the hearty loyalty He had earned so well! How have I treated Him? What do I mean to do henceforth?

You that love the Lord, hate evil.

—Ps. xcvi, 10.

* * *

Who shall separate us from the love of Christ? Shall tribulation? or distress? or famine? or nakedness? or danger? or persecution? or the sword? . . .

In all these things we overcome, because of Him that hath loved us.

—Rom. viii, 35, 33.

* * *

The Lord keepeth all them that love Him.

—Ps. cxliv, 20.

THE SIXTH WORD FROM THE CROSS

"Jesus, therefore, when He had taken the vinegar, said: It is finished."

Our Saviour had asked in one of His parables: "Which of you having a mind to build a tower, doth not first sit down and reckon the charges that are necessary, whether he have wherewithal to finish it?" (Luke xiv, 28). Christ our Lord has reckoned the charges. It was a costly work He undertook; but He has not shrunk from the outlay. He has finished it and paid for it with the last drop of His heart's blood; and now He can say with truth: "I have finished the work which Thou gavest Me to do."

Divine Love can do no more. One drop of this blood would have been too great a price for the whole world, and He has spent it all; "for with Him there is plentiful redemption." All the prophecies and types are fulfilled. The Paschal Lamb has been sacrificed. The Son of man has been lifted up, as the serpent was in the desert, for the healing of the nations. He has been "wounded for our iniquities and bruised for our sins." They have pierced His hands and feet; they have numbered all His bones. *It is finished.*

THE PRECIOUS BLOOD

Many daring things have been said of the glorious price of our salvation—the precious blood of Jesus Christ, but none in which the faint heart, sick of the world, of sin, and of self, can find more comfort than in the bold security with which the great St. Ignatius declares in his Spiritual Exercises: "When you present at the divine judgment-seat this price of your ransom, the precious blood, you are, therefore, paying more than you really owe." Who among us has not at times been terrified at the thought of the great unknown eternity? Who has not dreaded the solemn hour which will usher us into the presence of Him whom we love, oh! so tenderly, but whom we also fear so deeply, since in His hands are the issues of life and death.

Then, like the calm that fell on the troubled waters at the sound of His "Peace, be still," so over our affrighted souls flow the waves of the precious blood, its crimson streams effacing the handwriting on the wall which so haunts us, and bearing us in safety to the desired heaven. Let us dwell long and seriously on the words which have been re-echoing through the centuries since the days of St. Paul, "God who is rich in mercy." Our God, our very own, therefore His riches are ours, since "of His fulness we have all received." Why art thou sad, oh! my soul, and why dost thou disquiet me? From how many anxious hearts does not the plaint arise in words heard only in the sufferings and silence of the inner consciousness unfollowed by the sweet Hope in God, for I will still give praise to Him who is the salvation of my countenance and my God!

Oh! how little we know the graces that are fast closing in around us because of this laver of healing which is flowing in such copious streams from those dear founts in the hands and feet and side of our blessed Saviour.

Let us press our lips to those sacred wounds of our own making, and be comforted in the meditations of the twilight hour, that in His own royal way He will make them our refuge. They will be our "hollow places in the wall," where we may hide ourselves, safe from the shadow of distrust. Let us ask our blessed Mother, who is the treasure house of the riches of His mercy, and delighted in our claim of being her children, to intercede for us. Her love for us, more tender than that of a mother, will be the unfailing solace of life's darkest hours, and while the darkness gathers we will fain believe that her dear eyes will shine brightly through the gloom, and happy tears will well up at the thought of her who is "our life, our sweetness and our hope."

An Offering

Eternal Father, we offer Thee the blood, the passion and the death of Jesus Christ, the sorrows of Mary most holy, and of St. Joseph, in satisfaction for our sins, in aid of the holy souls in purgatory, for the needs of holy Mother Church, and for the conversion of sinners.

Ejaculations

Mary sorrowing, Mother of all Christians, pray for us.
Mary our hope, have pity on us.

* * *

God so loved the world, as to give His only-begotten Son; that whosoever believeth in Him, may not perish, but may have life everlasting.

For God sent not His Son into the world, to judge the world, but that the world may be saved by Him.

—*John iii, 16, 17.*

The Seventh Word From the Cross

"Jesus crying with a loud voice said: Father, into Thy hands I commend My spirit."

The cloud of desolation has passed away. The heavenly Father is looking down with infinite love on that beloved Son in whom He is well pleased. In peace in the selfsame He shall sleep and He shall rest; for Thou, O Lord, singularly hast settled Him in hope

(Ps. iv). "Did you not know that I must be about My Father's business?" (Luke ii, 49) are the first recorded words of our good Jesus, and these are the last: "My work is finished. Father, into Thy hands I commend My spirit." Grant me, dear Lord, to be zealous for the glory of my God, that with my last breath I may be able to resign my soul into His keeping with the love and confidence of a good son going home to his father.

"And, bowing His head, He gave up the ghost." St. John Chrysostom points out that, if a dying man's head is propped up, first death takes place and then the head falls forward by its own weight, the spirit of life being no longer there to support it. With Our Saviour it is not so. He first bows His head and then gives up the ghost, to show that He dies of His own will. "I lay down My life," He tells us, "that I may take it again. No man taketh it away from Me; but I lay it down of Myself; and I have power to lay it down, and I have power to take it up again" (John x, 17). What return can I make for a love like this? "He hath loved me, and hath delivered Himself for me" (Gal. ii, 20). "Greater love than this no man hath that a man lay down his life for his friends" (John xv, 13).

The death of Christ has taken all death's bitterness away; for "As Moses lifted up the serpent in the desert, so must the Son of man be lifted up; that whosoever believeth in Him may not perish, but may have life everlasting" (John iii, 14, 15).

"God sent not His Son into the world to judge the world but that the world may be saved by Him" (John iii, 17).

Prayer

Divine Jesus, incarnate Son of God, Who for our salvation didst vouchsafe to be born in a stable, to pass Thy life in poverty, trials, and misery, and to die amid the sufferings of the cross, I entreat Thee in the hour of my death, say to Thy divine

Father: *"Father, forgive him"*; say to Thy beloved Mother: *"Behold thy son"*; say to my soul: *"This day thou shalt be with Me in Paradise."* My God, my God, forsake me not in that hour. *"I thirst"* truly, my God, my soul thirsts after Thee, Who art the fountain of living waters. My life passes like a shadow; yet a little while and all will be consummated. Wherefore, my adorable Saviour, from this moment, for all eternity, *"Into Thy hands I commend my spirit."* Lord Jesus, receive my soul. Amen.

THE PIERCING OF CHRIST'S SIDE

"When they saw that He was already dead they did not break His legs; but one of the soldiers with a spear opened His side, and immediately there came out blood and water."

"And behold, the veil of the Temple was rent in two from the top even to the bottom, and the earth quaked and the rocks were rent.... Now the centurion and they that were with him watching Jesus, having seen the earthquake and the things that were done, were sore afraid, saying: Indeed, this was the Son of God."

All Nature bears witness to its dead Lord, the pagan Romans confess Him, the people go home smiting their breasts, and yet their priests and elders are unmoved. They besought Pilate that the legs of the crucified might be broken and that their bodies might be taken away.

But it is written of Christ, under the type of the paschal lamb: "Neither shall you break a bone thereof" (Ex. xii, 46). It is written again: "They shall look upon Me, whom they have pierced" (Zach. xii, 10). So one of the soldiers opened His side with a spear. Deep and wide was the wound the broad lance-head made; St. Thomas later on could put his hand into it. That wound has laid open to us the burning Heart of Our Redeemer, that, entering in, we may know how much He has loved us and learn to love Him in return.

"And immediately there came out blood and water," the water, as the Fathers teach, being a symbol of Baptism, the blood of the mystery of the altar; and so the Church is brought forth from the side of Christ, now asleep in death, just as Eve from the side of the sleeping Adam.

Let us kneel down and adore the dead body of our God and Saviour, thanking Him from our hearts for all He has done for us. What He really looked like we hardly dare to think. If our crucifixes showed Him as He was we should turn sick and look another way. "We have thought Him, as it were, a leper, and as one struck by God and afflicted. But He was wounded for our iniquities, He was bruised for our sins, the chastisement of our peace was upon Him, and by His stripes we are healed" (Is. liii, 4).

Yet we can take up a crucifix and examine it, discuss the pose of the limbs, the expression of the face, treat it, in fact, as a mere work of art and lay it down without a sigh!

Prayer Before a Crucifix

Look down upon me, good and gentle Jesus, while before Thy face I humbly kneel, and with burning soul pray and beseech Thee to fix deep in my heart lively sentiments of faith, hope, and charity, true contrition for my sins and a firm purpose of amendment; and while I contemplate with great love and tender pity Thy five wounds, pondering over them within me, and calling to mind the words which David, Thy prophet, said of Thee, my Jesus: "They have pierced My hands and My feet: they have numbered all My bones" (Ps. xxi, 17, 18).

THE ENTOMBMENT

"Joseph of Arimathea besought Pilate that he might take away the body of Jesus. And Pilate gave leave. He came therefore and took away the body of Jesus.

"And Nicodemus also came (he who at the first came to Jesus by night), bringing a mixture of myrrh and aloes, about an hundred pound weight.

"They took therefore the body of Jesus and bound it in linen clothes, with the spices, as the manner of the Jews is to bury.

"Now there was in the place where He was crucified a garden: and in the garden a new sepulchre, wherein no man yet had been laid.

"There, therefore, because of the parasceve of the Jews, they laid Jesus: because the sepulchre was nigh at hand."

—*John xix, 38-42*.

With sympathy and love for the bereaved Mother of Jesus, stand by and watch the little band of disciples as they perform this last solemn office over their beloved Master. The wounds in His hands have become so enlarged by the great weight upon them, that the hands can be drawn over the nails, without any great effort; but the nails through His feet must be forced out. Oh, how deep they have gone into the wood! At last they are loosened and removed, and then gently and reverently they lower the body of Our Saviour to the ground and lay His head on His Mother's breast.

Now they wash those gaping wounds and, taking off the thorny crown—though many of the thorns are embedded so deep that they can not be drawn out—they cleanse the filth and blood from His sacred face and, laying His arms by His sides, they swathe Him in His winding-sheet. When He came on earth He was wrapped in swaddling-clothes and laid in a manger; now He is to be laid in His tomb.

The holy Virgin has wept in silence till now; but now see how she sobs, poor broken-hearted Mother! She tries to take out those thorns fastened in His brow; but her tears blind her and she has to leave it to others. She is thinking of Him as He slept on her bosom at Bethlehem, as a boy at Nazareth, so beautiful, so lovable, so dear to God and to men. For more than thirty years she has foreseen the pitiful end of it all, and now it has come; her Jesus lies dead in her arms. "O all ye that pass by the way, attend, and see if there be any sorrow like my sorrow" (Lam. i, 12).

And all this is my doing! My sins demanded this awful atonement! How can Mary ever forgive me? Yet Jesus, I know, has forgiven me and with His last breath bequeathed her to me as my own mother. So I mingle my tears of penitence with her tears of love, knowing that she will be a mother to me.

And now they lift up the sacred body of the Saviour and carry it to the sepulchre hewn out of the rock. There they lay it down for the angels to take charge of till the hour of its glorious resurrection. They close the entrance with a great stone and go their ways, never to forget this hour with all its heart-rending sorrow, never to forget the divine Friend, who, "having loved His own who were in the world, loved them unto the end" (John xiii, 1).

Mater Dolorosa

There is a group of statuary called the "Pieta," which reminds us of all the sorrow of the Blessed Virgin, not by representing them all, but by presenting to our view that scene in the sacrifice of Calvary wherein the dead body of the Saviour, after having been taken down from the cross, is laid in the arms of the Mother of Sorrows; that moment when Mary gave to Jesus the last sad look and the last loving embrace ere His sacred body was consigned to the tomb. When we behold the dead body of Christ pressed to the bosom of the Virgin Mother, when we behold Mary's searching, agonizing glance into the sightless eyes, and into the gaping wounds of Jesus, we need not be told what had been, up to this, the Son's sufferings or the Mother's sorrows. Just as the last kiss on the brow of a loved one cold in death brings, in an instant, before the mind, the incidents of his last sickness, even the whole life of the dead, so one look on this group recalls all the incidents of Our Lord's suffering and of Our Lady's sorrow, with the distinctness and vividness with which a flash of lightning reveals objects in the darkness.

That we may learn how hard it is to form any adequate idea of Mary's sorrow, the Church applies to her the words of the prophet Jeremias: "To what shall I compare thee, or to what shall I liken thee, O daughter of Jerusalem? To what shall I equal thee, that I may comfort thee, O Virgin Daughter of Sion? For, great as the sea is thy destruction" (Lam. ii, 13).

Let those who would form some idea of her compassion look at Mary, from the moment of the Incarnation, standing in spirit as truly under the shadow of the cross as when she actually stood by the cross of Jesus on Mount Calvary. During that more than thirty years of martyrdom, her knowledge of Jesus' sufferings did not increase, but her realization of them became more and more vivid and painful in proportion as she saw Jesus increase in age, in wisdom, and in grace, until she saw Him offered a bleeding, dying Victim on the tree. Every time she saw Jesus, every time she heard Him, every time she thought of Him, she was compelled in spirit to offer Him as a propitiation for the sins of the world.

The Shadow of the Cross

There is a painting which may be called "The Shadow of the Cross." It represents a scene in the workshop of Nazareth. Joseph is employed at the carpenter's bench, Mary sits plying the distaff. A bright summer's day pours a flood of light into the room. Jesus, a beautiful youth, with filial piety informing every feature, advances with outstretched arms toward His Mother to embrace her, and to imprint a kiss upon her cheek. Oh, what would this scene have been to Mary, with what joy would it have dilated her soul, if only the future had been concealed from her! But, alas! looking at Jesus, the Mother's joy is turned into grief, because she sees that the loving attitude of her Son casts the shadow of the cross on the opposite wall.

What more touching, entrancing, than the scene enacted at Bethlehem! The winter winds were joyful with the music of the multitude of the heavenly host, praising God and singing "Glory to God in the highest, and peace on earth to men of good will"; the dismal cave was lighted up with the glory of heaven; angels, and wondering, adoring shepherds came to worship the new-born Saviour; and Mary and Joseph lovingly, adoringly, contemplated the heavenly Babe. Had that scene, which has filled the earth for centuries with light and gladness, no joy for Mary? Did not its splendor, for the time being, dispel the shadow of the cross? Did not Mary, in the words of Holy Scripture, rejoice Because a man was born into the world, and, for the moment, turn the eye of her soul from the vision of Calvary?

The Vision of Calvary

Alas! no. The joyous light of the Nativity only projected the shadow of the cross more distinctly upon Bethlehem. The scene in the stable, it is true, touched Mary's soul, caused rivers of love to well out of her heart, but only that the thought of Calvary might instantly change them into an ocean of bitterness. As Mary laid the divine Infant in the manger, as she saw His little arms stretch out as if to embrace her, she thought of the time that same Jesus would be laid upon the cross and nailed to it, when His arms would be stretched out in crudest torture, in infinite love, to embrace the whole human race. As she listened to the song of the angels, she thought of the blasphemies with which men would demand His death; as she looked on the reverent shepherds, she thought of the wild beasts that would cry for His blood; as she looked on the glory of heaven lighting the first opening of His eyes, she thought of the darkness that would fall upon their closing. As she saw earth and heaven rejoicing over His birth, she thought of how man and God would forsake Him at death, as she clasped Him to her bosom, she thought of the time when He would be laid at last, as you see Him in his group of statuary, all bleeding and bruised, wounded and lifeless, on her breast. Thus, even at Bethlehem, Mary stood in the shadow of the cross; and there, amid all the joy of that scene, was compelled to consecrate the winsome Infant to the death of Calvary....

Considering the intensity, bitterness, and duration of her sufferings in soul and body, the question arises: Could mortal have made greater sacrifices, or have suffered more in behalf of any cause, than Mary made and suffered by consenting to give her Son for the salvation of men? What did patriarch, or prophet, or apostle do for the salvation of men in comparison with what Mary suffered for it? If those who, at Christ's invitation, abandoned their nets and boats to follow Him, shall hereafter sit on thrones and judge the world, what must be Mary's place in the kingdom of God, since she, in obedience to the divine will (to appropriate the words of St. Paul), "spared not her own Son, but delivered Him up for us all"?

Let the redeemed learn, then, what they owe to Mary. Let them think of her more than thirty years' martyrdom, in consequence of her maternal instincts leading her to desire that the chalice of suffering might pass from her divine Son, while her obedience to the divine counsels and her devotion to man's salvation, doing a holy violence to her love, forced her to say: "Let the will of the Father be done; let my Son suffer death to redeem His people from their sins!"

Let them look often and thoughtfully upon the scene on Mount Calvary! Let them meditate on Mary's holy heroism. Let them think of her as a mother wounded in her tenderest affections; as sorrowful unto death, yet tearless; unwavering in her purpose to fulfill the promise made to God through Gabriel; willing to drain the chalice of her affliction; calm, when it came to making the sacrifice required for the redemption of the world; resolved to witness the end, to see Jesus blot out the hand-writing against sinners with the most precious blood He had drawn from the fountains of her heart; to stand by the cross until she heard: "Consummatum est,"—"It is finished"; until she saw her Son become the Saviour of the world, and the children of wrath become the children of God; until Jesus' lifeless body enfolded to her breast left her, amid the shadows of Calvary, in a desolation so unutterable that earth has no name for its anguish.

Let Christians look upon Mary crowned by Jesus on Calvary, in the words of Isaias, "with the crown of tribulation," and then they will understand why Mary takes an interest in their spiritual welfare; why she jealously guards the affair of their salvation in life; why she bends all her energies at the hour of death, to protect souls from the assault of the demon. Then they will understand why that unfailing devotion to the cause of the world's redemption which Mary displayed from Nazareth to Calvary she now exhibits in behalf of each and every one of the redeemed: to the end that the precious blood of Jesus shall not have been shed for any soul in vain.

—*Vide "Sermons" by Very Reverend D. I. McDermott, D.D.*

* * *

Now if we be dead with Christ, we believe that we shall live also together with Christ. . . .

So do you also reckon, that you are dead to sin, but alive unto God, in Christ Jesus our Lord.

—*Rom. vi, 8, 11.*

For the grace of God our Saviour hath appeared to all men;

Instructing us, that, denying ungodliness and worldly desires, we should live soberly, and justly, and godly in this world.

Looking for the blessed hope and coming of the glory of the great God and our Saviour Jesus Christ.

Who gave Himself for us, that He might redeem us from all iniquity, and might cleanse to Himself a people acceptable, a pursuer of good works.

—*Titus ii, 11-14.*

The Risen Lord and His Mother

The Gospels say nothing of this apparition; but common sense tells us that, as none was so dear to Our Lord as His holy Mother, none had been so faithful to Him, He could not fail to hasten first to gladden her with the joy of His resurrection. The Blessed Virgin knew that her Lord would rise again; her faith never wavered for a moment, and as He left Limbo for the sepulchre a deep peace come down upon her soul. When He raised His body to life she was conscious of it and her heart thrilled with deep and tender joy. She knew well that He would come first of all to visit her.

All at once her Jesus stands beside her. She clasps His feet and kisses them; then raising her from the ground He takes her in His arms, while she weeps for very gladness.

What a moment this for that blessed Mother! a foretaste of heavenly joy, making up for all she has gone through. "In the evening weeping shall have place, and in the morning gladness" (Ps. xxix 6). "According to the multitude of my sorrows in my heart, Thy comforts have given joy to my soul" (Ps. xciii, 19).

Let me take part in Mary's joy and thankfulness.

*　*　*

"My soul doth magnify the Lord. And my spirit hath rejoiced in God my Saviour."

—Luke, i, 46-47.

Regina Coeli

> O Queen of heaven, great joy to thee, Alleluia;
> For Jesus Christ who deigned to be, Alleluia,
> Thy child, is risen as He said, Alleluia.
> Pray bless all for whom He bled, Alleluia.
> V. Rejoice and be glad, O Virgin Mary, Alleluia;
> R. For the Lord is risen indeed, Alleluia.

Let us pray

O God, who didst vouchsafe to give joy to the world through the resurrection of Thy Son, our Lord Jesus Christ, grant, we beseech Thee, that through His Mother, the Virgin Mary, we may obtain the joys of everlasting life. Through the same Christ our Lord. Amen.

THE FIVE WOUNDS OF CHRIST

Our Lord has shown in His risen body that He means to retain His wounds forever.

Our Saviour retains His wounds for three reasons: *First,* as a memorial of His love and a pledge that He will never forget us. "Can a woman forget her infant, so as not to have pity on the son of her womb? And if she should forget, yet will not I forget thee. Behold, I have graven thee in My hands" (Is. xlix, 15). So in Catholic countries the crucifix is seen everywhere, not only in churches and in the houses of the faithful, but in marketplaces and law-courts, on the high-roads and in the mountain-passes, that the memory of Christ's love for us may be kept forever green and the thought of His sufferings be ever with us. Only the heretic, the infidel, and the devil would destroy it.

I will pray that the Faith of old may thrive and blossom and Christ reign supreme.

Secondly, that He may plead with them to His heavenly Father. To Noe God said: "I will set My bow in the clouds, and it shall be the sign of a covenant between Me, and between the earth: and when I shall cover the sky with clouds, My bow shall appear in the clouds; and I will remember My covenant with you and with every living soul that beareth flesh, and there shall no more be waters of a flood, to destroy all flesh" (Gen. ix, 13). Much more, then, is God moved to mercy when He looks on the wounds of His beloved Son. "Behold, O God, our protector, and look on the face of Thy Christ" (Ps. lxxxiii, 10). "If any man sin we have an advocate with the Father, Jesus Christ, the just" (1 John ii, 1).

Thirdly, that these blessed wounds may stir our hearts to gratitude, loyalty, and atonement. "And they shall say to Him: What are these wounds in the midst of Thy hands? And He shall say: With these I was wounded in the house of them that loved Me" (Zach. xiii, 6). "Behold this Heart," said Our Lord to Saint Margaret Mary, "which has loved men so much and is so little loved in return." These sacred wounds at the last day will fill the just with hope and joy; but what terror they will bring to the wicked! "They shall look on Me whom they have pierced" (Zach. xii, 10).

PART IV.
HUMAN SUFFERING

Motives for Patience

In your sufferings and afflictions reflect upon these three points: first, upon what we have deserved by our sins, and how very little we suffer in comparison with what we ought to suffer if we had our deserts; secondly, upon the sufferings the Son of God endured for our sins out of pure love for us, and the patience with which He endured them; thirdly, on the holy will of God, Who sends us these sufferings, and sends them for our greater good; Who knows what is best for us, and orders all things for the best if we leave ourselves to Him. Ah! how vain it is for us to resist His mighty hand! How foolish and sinful not to submit "to the dispositions of Him that is infinitely wise and infinitely good"!

* * *

We account them blessed who have endured. You have heard of the patience of Job, and you have seen the end of the Lord, that the Lord is merciful and compassionate.
—*James v, 11.*

In your patience you shall possess your souls.
—*Luke xxi, 19.*

Human Suffering

The right view of suffering is that of an expiation, not only for our own sin, but for the world's sin too. It is an expiation and a redemption, whereby the effects of sin are wiped away, and the creation is again to become a kingdom of God. All suffering centers in the supreme tragedy of Calvary, and when borne in a Christian spirit may be called a continuation of that divine sacrifice whereby the world is cleansed of its stain.

Wherefore as regards those who suffer: if they rebel against their lot, they are as those who deny their corporate responsibility and shirk their burden; they are traitors not only to the divine Redeemer, but to all suffering humanity. But if they accept the chalice of pain as Christ accepted it, they become truly compeers with Christ in the new kingdom of God, "sitting at His right hand and at His left," according to their merit. These are truly the co-workers of Our Saviour in the regeneration of the world. The innocent babe that dies in agony gains something of the martyr's glory; its suffering is the payment of a debt not its own, and yet its own because it is one of mankind; and it becomes more closely allied to Christ because of its suffering. The man or woman consciously accepting the cross, with perhaps its nameless horrors, becomes thereby a leader among men, because bearing willingly the burden of men; and according to the simplicity of their acceptance is the degree of their eternal glory. No wonder then that so many Christians have regarded it as a privilege to suffer, and have envied those who suffered, not from morbid sentiment, but from a healthy recognition of Christian principles. "These are they who have washed their garments in the blood of

the Lamb. Their youth is renewed like that of the eagle, as the lily shall they flourish in the city of the Lord."
—*Father Cuthbert, O.S.F.C., De Torrente.*

* * *

My brethren, count it all joy, when you shall fall into divers temptations;

Knowing that the trying of your faith worketh patience.

And patience hath a perfect work; that you may be perfect and entire, failing in nothing.
—*James i, 2-4.*

MY CHALICE INDEED YOU SHALL DRINK

Commenting on the words of Jesus to His disciples; "My chalice indeed you shall drink," Father Gallwey, S.J., writes in "The Watches of the Passion:" "To His chosen ones, to those to whom He afterward said, 'I will not now call you servants, but I have called you friends,' the grand and special promise that He makes is this: 'You shall, I promise you, before you die, drink of My chalice.' To His own most blessed Mother, as they conversed together in Nazareth, this, doubtless, was the assurance that He often repeated in order to console her, that she should be with Him to the end, and share His bitter chalice to the dregs. His golden promise afterward to St. Paul was, 'I will show him how great things he must suffer for My name's sake' (Acts, ix, 16).

"How blind, then, are we if we believe that every suffering is a calamity and a proof of God's wrath, and that prosperity is a sure sign of His favor!

"(a) He sends suffering in His mercy to atone here for past sin, to do here quickly the slow work of purgatory;

"(b) He sends suffering also to prevent sin, and to draw us out of sin, as suffering brought the prodigal home to Him;

"(c) Lastly, He sends suffering to His chosen ones as to St. Paul; and these chosen ones then become, like Himself, Saviours unto many."

As a strong antiseptic prevents the growth of germs of disease, so suffering checks the taint of base and selfish feelings, which so easily insinuate themselves into our hearts, and impair the purity of our motives and intentions. Suffering chastens the soul and its aspirations, the mind and its views, the heart and its affections. Whatever tends to free us from selfish motives must help to increase the merit of our thoughts, words, and actions.

Suffering increases merit by insuring not only greater purity, but also greater earnestness of motive. It has a bracing influence upon the will, and gives tone and vigor to its exercise. Difficulties and sufferings bring out manliness and strength of will and nobility of soul. They try earnestness of purpose. They are an unmistakable test of solid virtue. There is beauty and merit in each least aspiration of virtue breathed on the playful wing of joy, but there is greater and more solid merit in the depth and vigor of determination evinced in the practice of virtue under difficulties, temptations and trials. There is no trial, temptation, or suffering which cannot be turned into a blessing by the will of a conscious sufferer.

—*Egger: God and Human Suffering.*

* * *

Expect the Lord, do manfully, and let thy heart take courage, and wait thou for the Lord.

—*Ps. xxvi, 14.*

Do ye manfully, and let your heart be strengthened, all ye that hope in the Lord.

—*Ps. xxx, 25.*

THE ROYAL WAY: THE WAY OF THE CROSS

To many this seems a hard saying: "Deny thyself, take up thy cross, and follow Jesus" (Matt. xvi, 24).

But it will be much harder to hear that last word: "Depart from Me, ye cursed, into everlasting fire" (Matt. xxv, 41).

For they that at present willing hear and follow the word of the cross shall not then be afraid of eternal condemnation.

Take up, therefore, thy cross and follow Jesus, and thou shalt go into life everlasting.

He is gone before thee carrying His own cross; and He died for thee upon the cross that thou mayest also bear thy cross and love to die on the cross.

Because if thou die with Him thou shalt also live with Him, and if thou art His companion in suffering thou shalt also partake in His glory (2 Cor. i, 7).

Behold the cross is all, and in dying to thyself all consists, and there is no other way to life and to true internal peace but the holy way of the cross and of daily mortification.

Go where thou wilt, seek what thou wilt, and thou shalt not find a higher way above, nor a safer way below than the way of the holy cross.

Dispose and order all things according to thy will and as seems best to thee, and thou wilt still find something to suffer, either willingly or unwillingly, and so thou shalt still find the cross. For either thou shalt feel pain in thy body or sustain in thy soul tribulation of spirit. Sometimes thou shalt feel abandoned by God, at other times thou shalt be afflicted by thy neighbor, and what is more, thou shalt often be a trouble to thyself. Nor canst thou be released or relieved by any remedy or comfort, but needs must bear it as long as God wills.

For God would have thee learn to suffer tribulation without comfort, and wholly submit thyself to Him and to become more humble by tribulation.

No man hath so lively a feeling of the passion of Christ as he who hath happened to suffer such like things.

The cross, therefore, is always ready and everywhere waits for thee.

Thou canst not escape it, whithersoever thou runnest; for whithersoever thou goest thou carriest thyself with thee and shalt always find thyself.

Turn thyself upward, or turn thyself downward; turn thyself without, or turn thyself within thee, and everywhere thou shalt find the cross.

And everywhere thou must of necessity have patience, if thou desirest inward peace and wouldst merit an eternal crown.

If thou carry the cross willingly, it will carry thee and bring thee to thy desired end—to that place where there will be an end of suffering, though here there will be no end. If thou carry it unwillingly, thou makest it a burden to thee, and loadest thyself the more, and nevertheless thou must bear it. If thou fling away one cross, without doubt thou shalt find another and perhaps a heavier.

Dost thou think to escape that which no mortal ever could avoid? What saint was there ever in the world without his cross and affliction? Our Lord Jesus Christ Himself was not for one hour of His life without the anguish of His passion. "It behooved," said He, "that Christ should suffer, and rise from the dead, and so enter into His glory."

And how dost thou seek another way than this royal way, which is the way of the holy cross? The whole life of Christ was a cross and a martyrdom, and dost thou seek rest and joy?
—*Thomas à Kempis, The Following of Christ.*

* * *

What glory is it, if committing sin, and being buffeted for it, you endure? But if doing well, you suffer patiently; this is thankworthy before God.

For unto this are you called: because Christ also suffered for us, leaving you an example, that you should follow His steps.

Who did no sin, neither was guile found in His mouth.

Who, when He was reviled, did not revile: when He suffered, He threatened not: but delivered Himself to him that judged Him unjustly.
—*1 Peter ii, 20-23.*

* * *

He that saith he abideth in Him, ought himself also to walk, even as He walked.
—*1 John ii, 6.*

SKULL AND CROSS-BONES AT THE FOOT OF THE CRUCIFIX

Behold the skull and cross-bones at the foot of the crucifix; what is the origin and meaning of this representation? *The American Ecclesiastical Review* answers this question: "According to a very old tradition (Detzel, *Iconographie,* c. iv., p. 422), Adam, the father of the human race, was buried on the spot where Our Lord died. A similar tradition has it that a sprig of the tree of life which Adam took from paradise and planted as a lasting remembrance of his transgression in the place where he wished to be buried, became the wood from which the cross of Our Saviour was fashioned. Thus the tomb of Adam was identified with the spot on the mount of Calvary on which the cross was raised. So art has represented it for centuries, and the skull and bones of our first parents are placed there to indicate that they (and the whole race of men) receive new life through the death of Christ: '*Ecce resurgit Adam cui dat Deus in cruce vitam.*' (Inscript, cruc., in the Cathedral of Chur, in St. Ulricus at Augsburg, etc.)"

Pray and make sacrifices for the conversion of the whole human race; for love of Jesus crucified aid the Society for the Propagation of the Faith. There are in the world over one thousand millions of men and women in pagan and non-Catholic countries who are laboring in darkness and the shadow of death, who do not love the Sacred Heart of Jesus, because they do not know Him. Jesus thirsts for souls. For love of the Sacred Heart help and interest others in the work of Catholic missions.

*　*　*

Have mercy upon us, O God of all, and behold us, and show us the light of Thy mercies:

And send Thy fear upon the nations, that have not sought after Thee: that they may know that there is no God beside Thee, and that they may show forth Thy wonders.

Lift up Thy hand over the strange nations, that they may see Thy power.

For as Thou hast been sanctified in us in their sight, so Thou shalt be magnified among them in our presence,

That they may know Thee, as we also have known Thee, that there is no God beside Thee, O Lord.

Renew Thy signs, and work new miracles.
Glorify Thy hand, and Thy right arm.
—Ecclus. xxxvi, 1-7.

THE PROVIDENCE OF GOD

Not content with offering Himself to us as our last end, God, though respecting our free will, leads us by the hand to that blessed goal. His providence has accompanied us through all the paths of life until this very moment. Nothing in the world is abandoned to the caprice of chance. But all events, whatever they may be, take place:

1. in the sight of God; 2. by His permission; 3. in accordance with His providential plan.

NOTHING IS DONE EXCEPT IN THE SIGHT OF GOD

God, being infinite in His knowledge, sees everything. We should not represent Him as a king isolated and far removed beyond the world in the majestic solitude of His palace. No; on the contrary, He is intimately present to the beings He has created and still preserves by His almighty power.

To the loving, faithful soul, what does it matter that men forget it, misunderstand it, despise it, persecute it?

Is it not enough to know that God sees all and that in heaven there is a Witness whose eye nothing escapes?

"To them that love God all things work together unto good" (Rom. viii, 28).

* * *

"Good things and evil, life and death, poverty and riches, are from God."
—*Ecclus. xi, 14.*

Nothing Is Done Except by the Permission of God

To judge things superficially, it would seem that God is only an idle spectator of the events in the world. His hand is hidden except in some extraordinary circumstances, His activity in the world is not apparent: nevertheless, although hidden, the action of God is none the less real. While respecting the liberty of creatures, He rules the world according to His own pleasure. The wicked themselves, to whom God has given such astonishing power for evil, accomplish only what he allows them to do. God, while seeming to leave a free field to human activity, confines it within limits which it will never exceed. Even when it goes astray and gives itself up to the greatest excesses, it is ever subordinated to the supreme will that governs it, against which it can do nothing: which says to it: "Thou shalt go no further" (Job. xxxviii, 11).

This empire of God over human wills appears most striking in relation to the Church, which wicked men can attack, persecute, even seem to conquer. But they can never succeed in destroying it. It is on this foundation that the Church places its unshaken confidence in the midst of strifes; and we know this confidence will not be confounded.

* * *

"Woe to them that are faint-hearted, who believe not God: and therefore they shall not be protected by Him: Woe to them that have lost patience, and that have forsaken the right way."
—*Ecclus. ii, 15-16.*

* * *

"Take courage and fear not. God Himself will come and will save you."

—*Is. xxxv, 4.*

Nothing Happens Except in Fulfillment of the Providential Plan of God

Since He is infinitely wise, God can not do anything, can not even admit anything useless or superfluous in His works. With how much greater reason must He exclude anything that would be an obstacle to the ends that He has prescribed.

So everything in the world has its end, its usefulness, a reason for its existence. Thus it is in the physical world and could not be otherwise in the moral world. Doubtless God does not will everything in the same way. He approves what is good; and though tolerating evil, He forbids and condemns it. But since He admits both in His divine plan, He must have found the way to make them both serve the ends that He wills to attain and to make even sin contribute to the beauty and harmony of the universe.

As we well know, in the government of the world God has no other purpose but to sanctify His elect on earth that He may glorify them eternally in heaven. Such is the end that everything realizes after its own manner, and this is why the apostle could say very truly that everything cooperates for the good of those who love God.

Give me, O Lord, a more lively faith in the consoling truth of Thy providence. In all events, happy and unhappy, may I see and reverence that wise and adorable Providence, always so good and merciful, always deserving of my love. May I confide myself to thee, may I abandon myself entirely to Thee with all I have and all that I am, at present and in the future, for time and eternity. "Whether we live or whether we die, we are the Lord's" (Rom. xiv, 8).

—Branchereau: Meditations.

Conformity to the Will of God

Our whole perfection consists in loving our most amiable God, and all the perfection of the love of God consists in uniting our will with His most holy will. The greatest glory that we can give to God is to fulfil His blessed will in all things.

The pure and perfect love which the Blessed in heaven have for God, consists in the perfect union of themselves with His holy will.

Conformity means our joining our will with the will of God; uniformity means our making the divine will and our own will but one, so that we will nothing but what God wills, and God's will alone is our will. This is the summit of perfection to which we should always aspire; this should be the object of all our actions, of all our desires, meditations and prayers. If you embrace all things in life as coming from the hands of God, and even death to fulfil His holy will, assuredly you will die a saint and will be saved. Let us then abandon ourselves in all things to the good will of that Lord, who, being most wise, knows what is best for us, and being most loving, since He has given His life for the love of us, wills also what is best for us.

—St. Alphonsus Liguori.

* * *

It is the Lord; let Him do what is good in His sight.
—1 Kings iii, 18.

Whereas he (Tobias) had always feared God from his infancy, and kept His commandments, he repined not against God because the evil of blindness had befallen him,

But continued immovable in the fear of God, giving thanks to God all the days of his life.

—*Tob. ii, 13, 14.*

Suffering Is a Superior Form of Action

I know by experience, that certain graces are obtained for others in time of trial, graces which all our efforts could not previously obtain. Hence I have reached the conclusion that suffering is a superior form of action, the highest expression of the admirable Communion of Saints; and that in suffering we are sure of making no mistake (as we sometimes do in acting), sure also of being useful to others, and to the great causes which we dream of helping.

—*Elizabeth Leseur, Diary.*

* * *

The service of God and the service of souls; it is both of these that the crucified soul practises in imitation of Our Saviour; and her sufferings, continuing the passion of Jesus in His mystical body, complete it, as it were, according to the expression of St. Paul; thus becoming admirably fruitful for her personal sanctification, and for the conversion of others.

—*The Art of Christian Suffering.*

* * *

I fill up those things that are wanting to the sufferings of Christ, in my flesh, for His body, which is the Church.

—*Col. i, 24.*

Vicarious Suffering

St. Teresa suffered much, and she bore her sufferings with heroic patience.

When such a Saint as Teresa suffers, she suffers like Our Lord upon the cross, as an immaculate, innocent victim. But what could life offer her more sweet, more blissful than in this manner to resemble the Lamb of God, not merely in His innocence, but in His passion?

Now, we know that the angels laud and magnify God with songs of exultant joy, and man praises Him in thanksgiving for His benefits, but how few there are who, like the Son of God, raise the hymn of unceasing praise to the harp-notes of unmerited, vicarious suffering, as did St. Teresa! Praise to the Most High, when chanted to the minor key of pain and woe is surely the noblest tribute that can be rendered to Him. Finally, think upon this, my soul: if prayer, almsgiving, good works are subservient to the salvation of our fellow-men and obtain blessings for them, how much greater must be the power of intercessory, propitiatory suffering offered by some innocent soul on their behalf? If we believe St. Teresa to have conferred great benefits, unspeakably great benefits on her fellow-men, we may be certain that by far the largest amount of those blessings were earned for them upon her bed of pain. Now at last you will be able to understand the words of the Saint: The greater the tribulation, the greater the gain. Do you feel no desire for such gain? Let us hope that you will at least profit in this respect, by gaining a more elevated view of suffering, and more patience to bear suffering.

A Sinner Is Slowly Breathing Out His Life

Many a human being is this moment on his death-bed. On the cot of a hospital ward, in a den of sin, on the prairies of the West, in the woods of Africa, out on the rough waves of an ocean-storm, perhaps unknown, alone, unconscious, a sinner is slowly breathing out his life. A few moments more, and all will be over for a never-ending eternity. Oh, how many of the dying are dead in sin! how many there are whose souls are laden with a thousand deeds of darkness! how many cold and reckless, how many struggling in despair! Shall Our Lord's blood bear no ransom; shall His Heart have loved in vain; shall He be deprived of the glory that He so justly claims? Oh, pray with Him, suffer with Him. Have you the courage of love? Then offer yourself a victim to Him. Let the lamp of your life be burnt out for Him. Let sorrow darken your pathway and thorns be strewn over its sod. Let anguish of spirit be yours, since so often it was His. One day the good Master will meet you with a welcome and rest your weary head upon His bosom, and there let you be inebriated with the joy of His own living Heart.

* * *

The souls of the just are in the hand of God, and the torment of death shall touch them.

In the sight of the unwise they seemed to die: and their departure was taken for misery:

And their going away from us for utter destruction: but they are in peace.

And though in the sight of men they suffered torments, their hope is full of immortality.

—*Wis. iii, 1-4.*

But the just shall live for evermore: and their reward is with the Lord, and the care of them with the Most High.

—*Wis. v, 16.*

PART V.
HUMILITY AND PATIENCE

Humility

The virtue of humility is deemed by the saints the foundation and the safeguard of all the other virtues. Although holy humility may not be called the most distinguished among the virtues, yet, as St. Thomas says, it takes the first place, inasmuch as it is the foundation of the others. St. Augustine says that humility must accompany all our actions, must be with us everywhere; for as soon as we glory in our good works they are of no further value to our advancement in virtue.

Before the advent of Jesus Christ upon earth the beautiful virtue of humility was little known and little loved. It was even despised, because pride, the first cause of man's fall, dominated all. The Son of God, therefore, came down from heaven to teach it, not only by word, but also by His example. St. Basil, contemplating the life of the divine Saviour, shows that every moment of it, from His birth to His death, teaches us this particular virtue.

St. Augustine, speaking of the humility of Jesus, says: "If His humility does not free us from pride, I know of no other remedy." Writing to Dioscorus, he says: "Would you know, my friend, which is the virtue that makes us true disciples of Jesus Christ, and unites us intimately with God? Most emphatically I say it is humility. And as often as you ask me I shall tell you the same."

* * *

The foolish things of the world hath God chosen that He may confound the wise; and the weak things of the world hath God chosen that He may confound the strong. And the base things of the world, and the things that are contemptible, hath God chosen, and things that are not, that He might bring to naught things that are: that no flesh should glory in His sight.

—*1 Cor. i, 27-29.*

* * *

At that hour the disciples came to Jesus saying: Who thinkest Thou is the greater in the kingdom of heaven? And Jesus calling unto Him a little child, sat him in the midst of them. And said: Amen, I say to you, unless you be converted, and become as little children, you shall not enter into the kingdom of heaven. Whosoever, therefore, shall humble himself as this little child, he is the greater in the kingdom of heaven.

—*Matt. xviii, 1-4.*

* * *

For if any man think himself to be something, whereas he is nothing, he deceiveth himself.

—*Gal. vi, 5.*

* * *

Jesus called them to Him and said: You know that the princes of the Gentiles lord it over them; and they that are the greater exercise power upon them. It shall not be so among you; but whosoever will be the greater among you, let him be your minister.

And he that will be first among you, shall be your servant. Even as the Son of man is not come to be ministered unto, but to minister, and to give His life a redemption for many.
—*Matt. xx, 25-28.*

* * *

Take up My yoke upon you, and learn of Me, because I am meek, and humble of heart; and you shall find rest to your souls.
—*Matt. xi, 29.*

* * *

"Odibilis coram Deo et hominibus superbia" (Ecclus. x, 7). Pride is hateful before God and men.

* * *

"Erubescat homo esse superbus propter quem humilis factus est Deus."—St. Augustine. Man should be ashamed to be proud when he thinks how humble God became for him.

* * *

CHRIST THE MASTER OF HUMILITY

Nothing cramps the freedom of the soul in a greater degree than the fear of what others will think and say. The first thing to be done after taking the narrow way is to shut the world out of consideration and look only to the approval of God.

Humility so perfects man for God that when the Son of God took our nature He could find no other virtue so capable of uniting that nature with God.

* * *

When we speak of Christ as the Master of humility, we speak of something preeminently great and excelling. The Son of God could not take the nature of man without making that nature morally perfect, and He has shown in Himself that the foundation of moral perfection in a creature is perfect humility. He could not, again, take the office upon Him of our Mediator and Redeemer without showing us in a preeminent way by what virtue we are reconciled to God and made open to His sanctifying gifts. This virtue He therefore manifested the most conspicuously in Himself. He took it as His singular prerogative because it was the perfect subjection of His humanity to His divinity, because it was the virtue by which He redeemed the world, and because it is the one virtue by which every soul that He came to redeem returns to God. To this virtue, therefore, as to His great human prerogative, He especially appealed as to the chief lesson that we are to learn of Him, "Learn of Me, for I am meek and humble of heart."

* * *

Let it be further observed that in all His humble words and ways, our divine Lord never speaks directly of His own humility but once. He lives and breathes and personifies the virtue, as what is inseparable from Him; but of His own humility He spoke but once. He spoke once because that was necessary for our instruction; He spoke once to consecrate this wonderful virtue. He spoke only once because of the exceeding delicacy and hidden nature of the virtue, which, like purity, is far too modest to be spoken of by its possessor except in a case of absolute necessity. And in this, too, He conveys to us a profound instruction. "Come," He says, "to Me, learn of Me;" "I am the way, the truth, and the life; no man cometh to the Father except through Me" (John xiv, 6). He is the way to heaven, the truth from heaven, the life that brings heaven; and He says, Come to Me; learn this one thing from Me, and you shall know all things; learn this one thing from Me, and you shall possess all things; learn of Me to be meek and humble of heart. There is nothing so wonderful in power as the humility of Christ, who, resting the created nature of His humanity wholly upon His divine nature, ascribes nothing whatever to that human nature, which He knew so perfectly to be nothing without God.

Having once learned from Christ that the great lesson He has come to teach us is His own meekness and humility, we then discover that His incarnation, His birth, all the actions of His life, His sufferings and death, all speak to us, and breathe into us, this divine lesson of humility; and everywhere, even when His voice is silent, His life and conduct say to us: "Learn of Me, because I am meek and humble of heart."

* * *

The Passion of Christ Is the Book of Humility

The passion of Our Lord presents all the great virtues in their perfection for our imitation, whether self-denial, poverty of spirit, obedience, silence, humility, purity, patience, prayer, resignation, contempt of the world, or charity. But among all these virtues He preeminently appears as the Master of humility. His passion is the book of humility. His cross is the throne of humility, the terrible way from the Mount of Olives to Mount Calvary is the substantive exposition of the words, "Learn of Me, for I am meek and humble of heart."

The cross is the instrument of contrition upon which the earthly man is broken to be reformed upon the heavenly man. The cross is the divine school of patience; the school of self-abnegation; the school of penance; the school of charity. The foot of the cross, where Mary stood with John, and where the prostrate Magdalen wept her loving grief, is the great school of humility, where the soul is purified and brought to God. There forever sounds the great command of the divine Master: "Learn of Me, for I am meek and humble of heart."

"Empty yourself, and see that I am God" (Ps. lxxii, 20-28). Humility is the animated capacity of the soul, vacated of self-seeking, and looking to God with desire to be tilled with His light, grace and goodness.

God will not throw away His noble gifts upon those who cannot be made worthy of them even by the gifts themselves. If the soul is not subject to God as well as open, she cannot receive the grace of the Christian virtues.

Frail as man is, humility will make a foundation in him strong enough for God to raise an edifice upon it that shall last for eternity. The progress of humility is the progress of the soul. We may know the extent of the grace that is given us by the strength of our humility. Our very perfection is humility. The gifts and prerogatives conferred on the Blessed Virgin were all given to her humility; this she expressly declares in her Canticle of gratitude.

* * *

ONE UNCEASING ADMONITION IN THE HOLY SCRIPTURE

From the beginning to the end of the Holy Scriptures, we shall find, if we study them attentively, one fundamental truth, and one unceasing admonition. We hear it in Paradise, we see it on the cross. It runs through the sacred histories, is loud in the prophets, frequent in the sapiential books, continuous in the Gospels, and rises in many pages of the Apostolic writings. This fundamental truth instructs us to know, this constant admonition exhorts us to act on the belief, that what God accepts from man is humility, and that what He rejects is pride. His blessings are for the humble. His maledictions are for the proud. In every virtue it is humility that He rewards, in every vice it is pride that He punishes. And when we remember that it is humility that subjects the soul and the virtues to God, and that it is pride that sends the soul away from God, and inflames the vices with its malice, we shall see that it cannot be otherwise.

Let us, then, entreat of God with our whole powers, that in His mercy He would deliver us from pride, and would grant us the inestimable gift of humility, that we may not follow the evil spirits in their pride to destruction, but Christ, the divine Master of humility, to sanctification: which may God in His goodness grant us now and forever.

—*The Little Book of Humility and Patience*, by Archbishop Ullathorne.

Patience and Humility

So intimate is the connection between patience and humility, that neither of these virtues can make much progress without the other; nor can charity advance towards its perfection without their aid.

Patience is concerned in all that we have to resist, in all that we have to deny ourselves, in all that we have to endure, in all that we have to adhere to, and in all that we have to do. Wherever patience fails, the act is weak, and the work imperfect.

* * *

The first thing required to be understood is that patience is an immediate exercise of the will, which is the spring of all free and moral actions. It must not, therefore, be confounded with the sentiments, sensibilities or feelings, because it is a pure act of the will. When the will rests on God, looks to God and draws strength from God, that patience is generated which resists all evils and disorders, gives us the possession of ourselves, and keeps the soul in peace. "Be thou, O my soul, subject to God, for from Him is my patience" (Ps. lxi, 6).

The first movements of impatience, the first uneasiness of dissatisfaction, are warnings to patience to be upon its guard, lest trouble arise to disturb the soul and take hold of the will. If we calmly look down from the superior soul upon the first movements of irritation or impatience, nothing can appear more contemptible; and under the rebuke of the gaze of our interior eye they vanish in shame. The breath of patience will disperse the little cloud of trouble and discontent that moves in our lower nature, but if left to itself it will quickly grow on what it feeds upon, and will envelop and fill the soul with anger and vexation. For anger is a brooding vice that feeds on sensitive self-love and imaginary wrong far beyond the original offence, if, indeed, offence has been given.

There is nothing that drives us to impatience so vehemently, or throws us into great interior disorder, than an injury, or the imagination of an injury, which is far more frequent than real injury. For many things are said and done without the least intention of injury; some from quickness of tongue, some from inadvertence or thoughtlessness, some in good-natured jest, some from good intentions, some from mere imprudence; and no one has any right to take any of them in bad part, and so commit himself to anger, grief and sadness. But if any one should falsely or maliciously assail our good name and reputation—a mode of detraction not limited, alas! to the children of this world—let us in that case keep our magnanimity, that our virtue may be stronger than another's vice, and that our patience may suffer no loss by reason of another's improbity. Rather should we rejoice in the Lord that He has called us by these means to greater justice, which is commonly born, receives its growth, and obtains perfection among injuries and insults.

* * *

A fool immediately showeth his anger: but he that dissembleth injuries is wise.
—*Prov. xii, 16.*

* * *

As long as we are simple, upright, fearing God and departing from evil, placing our hope in God and not in the prudence of the world, He who has care of His servants will turn their calamities into blessings. The only good we have that is excellent and imperishable is our soul, and the good which God gives to the soul. But by nothing except our own will can the soul or its good suffer injury. No one can be spiritually injured except by himself. So long as one possesses one's soul in patience, no one can take any part of that good away from us. We can only lose the good of the soul by not holding to it with constancy, and we thus sin by losing patience.

* * *

Food is not more essential to strength of body than patience is to strength of soul; and God in His goodness makes us conscious of our weakness, that we may be induced to seek the means of strength. What God loves and approves in us is the cheerful and loving patience that we put into our duties, because that is the spirit of charity and expresses the amount of charity with which we serve Him. Every new restraint that we put upon the hurry and impetuosity of our excitable nature is a reduction to order, a power gained, a weakness removed, a further subjection of nature to grace, a step in the way of peace that makes us less unlike to God. The secret of cheerfulness and content is in the freedom of spirit obtained by the conquest of the body.

Jesus Christ the Teacher and Model of Patience

As the Lord of men, Jesus Christ became their teacher, and He exhorts us to take up our daily cross, and to follow Him with patience.

Severe to Himself, He is gentle, mild and forbearing to all others. His meekness is the beautiful flower. His peacefulness the sweet fruit of His patience. His doctrine is doubted and disputed; He is charged with being an impostor; He is called a blasphemer; His wonderful works are ascribed to the devil; His adversaries gnash their teeth, burn with rage and are prepared to stone Him. Yet His equanimity is unmoved, His meek demeanor is not altered, the calmness of His peace undergoes no change. Resting on His union with His Father, the ground of His invincible strength, His divine fortitude is tried at every point, and at every point His patience is invincible.

* * *

He calls upon us to be the imitators of His patience, to rest for strength on Him; to take up our daily cross and follow Him; to refrain from our selfish egotism; and in patience to possess our souls.

As the patient sufferings of Our Lord were the cause of His glory, the like patience in sufferings will bring us to His glory.

Patience As the Perfecter of Our Daily Actions

That perfection of life consists in doing our ordinary actions well is one of the wisest maxims of the saints. Those duties make up the chief sum of our lives during the time allotted to us in this world. As we owe our life and time to God, the good Christian has duties at all hours.

The perfection of our ordinary actions depends on high motives, good will and cheerful patience. High motives give them their value before God; good will makes them vigorous; cheerful patience makes them orderly, peaceful, effective, and pleasant. Hence the poor man who goes to his daily toils with good will and cheerful patience for the love of God is a much nobler person in the sight of God than the man who, from mere human motives, shines with splendid actions in the sight of the world.

* * *

Whatever we do is perfect in proportion to the self-possession with which we do it, and that self-possession is proportioned to patience. Nothing, however trifling, can be done well without good judgment. There are fifty ways of doing anything, but only one perfect way. Nature is always inclined to hurry, to run before judgment, but grace is deliberate. To work fruitfully is to work with a patient will; fretful haste damages both the work and the workman.

They who are patient with obstacles will be patient when the work runs smoothly.

There are few greater proofs of a well-disciplined interior than to be able to break off at any time with cheerfulness from one duty and to turn with equal cheerfulness to another, however unexpected the interruption may be. It is an effect of that detachment of will that comes of patient charity.

"In Your Patience You Shall Possess Your Soul"

There is nothing that we suffer for the honor of God, however little it may be, that is not more serviceable to us than if we possessed the dominion of the world. But suffering must be unselfish. God would not have us suffer anything for His sake that is not both useful and fruitful to ourselves. However great our trial or affliction may be, the Son of God bore them first, and permits them for our good.

Christ Our Lord not only perfected His own patience by His sufferings, but He receives all the sufferings endured by His members for His sake, incorporates them with His own, endows them with His merits, and thus gives them a communion with His own proportioned to their loving patience. For in virtue of His grace and love they are made sacred and holy.

* * *

We may sum up the value of patience and resigned suffering in the language of the devout and learned Blosius:

1. Nothing more valuable can befall a man than tribulation, when it is endured with patience for the love of God, because there is no more certain sign of the divine election. But this should be understood quite as much of internal as of external trials.

2. It is the chain of patient sufferings that forms the rings with which Christ espouses a soul of Himself.

3. There is such a dignity in suffering for God's sake, that we ought to account ourselves unworthy of an honor so great.

4. Good works are of great value; but even those lesser pains and trials that are endured with peace and patience are more valuable than many good works.

5. Every sorrowful trial bears some resemblance to the most excellent passion of Our Lord Jesus Christ, and when it is endured

with patience, it makes him who endures it a more perfect partaker of the passion of his Lord and Saviour.

6. Tribulation opens the soul to the gifts of God, and when they are received tribulation preserves them.

7. What we now suffer God has from eternity foreseen, and has ordained that we should suffer in this way, and not in any other way.

On the Cheerfulness of Patience

There can be no better proof of a healthy soul than habitual cheerfulness. Christian cheerfulness is that modest, hopeful, and peaceful joy which springs from charity and is protected by patience. It is the well-regulated vigor of spiritual life that throws off all morbid humors and depressing influences, refusing them a lodgment in the soul devoted to God. Cheerfulness gives freedom to our thoughts and a generous spirit to our actions. It makes our services to God acceptable, and our services to our neighbor grateful. "God loveth the cheerful giver" (2 Cor. ix, 7).

This cheerfulness of soul springs from the divine good which God has placed within us, which acts within us, and of which we are partakers. Hence purity of conscience is a great promoter of cheerfulness, for when the conscience is clean the affections are pure. But the moving cause of cheerfulness is in the exercise of the virtues, especially as they are the ready servants of the joy of loving God. Yet even the joy of charity is very imperfect, and is often troubled, unless that charity be patient.

* * *

Nothing contributes more to cheerfulness than the habit of looking at the good side of things. The good side is God's side of them. But even on their human side, what makes them appear worse than they are is conferred on them by the envy, jealousy and malice of our hearts, falsely imagining that what depresses others exalts ourselves. Let patience keep down envy and repress the fancy of our own superiority.

Cheerfulness implies hope, courage, confidence in God, the turning a deaf ear to the complaints of self-love, and a certain modest joy in the consciousness that in the hand of God, "in whom we live, and move, and have our being," we are safe.

Why should we not rejoice in the good things of God? We can rejoice in the good things of the senses, why not in the good things of the soul? If the day is pure and serene we enjoy its gladness. Why should we not rejoice in the serene light of truth that shines from Heaven upon our minds? Why should we not delight in the beautiful gifts of God? Having an Almighty and most loving Father, let us rejoice in Him. Having a most loving Saviour, very God of God, who has made Himself our brother, and feeds us with His life, we ought surely to rejoice in Him. Having the Holy Spirit of God with us, dwelling in us with wonderful condescension, making us His temples, and pouring His love into our hearts, we ought certainly to answer His love and rejoice in His overflowing goodness. Why should we ever set a gloomy face against a guest so beautiful and generous?

The great enemy of the soul is not trial but sadness, which is the bleeding wound of self-love.

"We may always rejoice," observes St. Chrysostom, "if we will only keep our head a little raised above the flood of human things."

* * *

As the saints and martyrs had their share in drinking of Our Saviour's cup of sufferings, so they have all "run with patience to the sight set before them; looking on Jesus, the author and finisher of faith, who having joy set before Him endured the cross" (Heb. xii, 1, 2). "They all in life possessed their souls in their patience" (Luke xxi, 19). They all in death saved their souls by patience. "Patience hath a perfect work," saith St. James i, 4, "that you may be perfect and entire, failing in nothing." "He that is patient," said the wise man, Prov. xiv, 29, "is governed with much wisdom." And again, Prov. xvi, 32, "the patient man is better than the valiant, and he that ruleth his spirit than he that taketh cities." Patience then is the virtue of the martyrs and of all the saints; patience made them martyrs and saints; patience made them perfect; patience brought them to that incorruptible crown, which is given to none but those who have fought for it and who have won it by their patient endurance on the way of the cross.

* * *

Resolve to pray and to labor earnestly that thou mayest acquire the virtue of patience; it will make all thy sufferings light and easy, and entitle them to an eternal reward. Whenever thou art visited with any cross, of what kind soever, always consider it as coming from the hand of God; presently accept it, and offer it up to Jesus Christ crucified, to be united to His sufferings, to be sanctified through Him, and accepted by His Father for His own greater glory, and the remission of thy sins. Happy shalt thou be if, under all thy sufferings, thou makest this thy practice!

* * *

For thou art my patience, O Lord: my hope, O Lord, from my youth.

—*Ps. lxx, 5.*

A patient man shall bear for a time, and afterwards joy shall be restored to him.

—Ecclus. i, 29.

* * *

The fruit of the Spirit is charity, joy, peace, patience, benignity, goodness, longanimity.

—Gal. v, 22.

Through Many Tribulations We Must Enter Into the Kingdom of God

In every walk in life there are trials; yet in every case we have to recognize the wisdom and goodness of God's providence for those who love Him. Untoward events have their place in the dispensations of Divine Providence in regard of the just; but the just may not readily perceive the wise reason of such events. Life is said to be a problem. Men often look in the wrong direction for the solution of this problem. Without seeking any solution of it, those who truly love God will also trust in Him, and will leave themselves in His hands. It may be said that all events have relation in some way to the well-being of God's elect. Even the crimes and machinations of the wicked may be permitted by God, in as far as they go for the trial of His servants. The world is not in its government subject to mere chance, but it falls under the Divine plan. In this plan, provision is made for all things, the wickedness of sinners having been fully foreseen. God does not, however, hand to us the key of His governmental plan; but He demands of us a dutiful confidence in His infinite wisdom, power, and goodness. We shall not deserve to be reckoned just if we refuse God this confidence.

Devout Christian, say with St. Paul: "O the depth of the riches of the wisdom and of the knowledge of God! How incomprehensible are His judgments, and how unsearchable His ways!" (Rom. xi, 33). Submit yourself willingly to God, even when He tries you with sufferings and contradictions. He knows what is best for you.

GOD KNOWS WHAT IS BEST FOR US

It is our duty to recognize, when nothing succeeds with us, when we suffer bereavement, when some dire calamity occurs, or when we have a visitation of sickness, that these untoward occurrences, just as happier ones, have their place in the Divine plan for our well-being and profit. The designs of God are not first submitted to men for their consideration and approval, but they are carried out in exercise of the Divine and most complete Sovereignty. To this Supreme Sovereignty the just readily and fully submit themselves, and herein is seen their justice. In this submission, too, is the foundation of their heavenly reward. In some cases the outcome of trials manifests to us even now what we shall recognize most evidently hereafter. Thus we find that often a visitation of sickness or a loss of fortune causes men to turn from an irreligious or scandalous life to one more in keeping with their duty to God. Sometimes God interposes by some unlikely or unexpected circumstance, when death is imminent, but when men are not prepared to die; and He thus saves them, and affords them time for repentance and amendment. Sometimes God permits, through some unpleasant misunderstanding, the breaking-off of a friendship: and this proves a manner of escape from an influence which might be fatal to someone's salvation. In such cases we see reason to bless God for His providence; why will we not extend our gratitude to other cases of trial? for we may be sure that God's wisdom and goodness mark all His dealings with us.

Devout Christian, in your trials say with Heli: "It is the Lord: let Him do what is good in His sight" (1 Kings iii, 18).

Trust in God's Providence

It is our duty to fall in with the Divine plan. God's way must be the right way. If the sky be overcast, and the road be rough, what will it matter, provided only that we are on the right way? Is is not written that "through many tribulations we must enter into the kingdom of God" (Acts xiv, 21)? If only we trust in God's providence firmly, our confidence will be to us a source of consolation and courage under the adverse occurrences of life. Would we foolishly trust in ourselves? Has not experience shown us how seldom the golden plans we formed for ourselves were realized? Were they not thwarted by a turn of the wheel of fortune, by sickness, by interference from without, and even by the inclemency of the weather? Why was there this failure? It was because our plans did not enter into the Divine plan. Let us then mistrust ourselves. We cannot but be right when we desire only God's good pleasure, and submit ourselves willingly to His dispensations. St. Paul assures us, saying: "To them that love God, all things work together unto good" (Rom. viii, 28). Say confidently with David: "The Lord ruleth me: and I shall want nothing" (Ps. xxii, 1).

* * *

Although He should kill me I will trust in Him.
—*Job xiii, 75.*

* * *

Now all chastisement for the present indeed seemeth not to bring with it joy, but sorrow; but afterwards it will yield, to them that are exercised by it, the most peaceable fruit of justice.
—*Heb. xii, 11.*

THE THOUGHT OF HELL A MOTIVE OF PATIENCE

When great evils oppress the sinner, the thought of hell ought to be a powerful motive of patience. Ought the sinner to complain of any evil, however great it may appear, when he realizes that he has deserved the pains of hell, that is to say, an infinite, an eternal evil? If a lost soul could exchange places with you, you who murmur on account of your evils, he would esteem himself happy; your state would be paradise to him. At present, your state seems a hell to you because you do not meditate on the pains of hell, nor fully realize that you have deserved hell as your portion. No suffering should appear unbearable to one who has deserved the pains of hell.

* * *

THE THOUGHT OF CALVARY A MOTIVE OF PATIENCE

The thought of Calvary should be a great motive of patience to a Christian. Compare your sufferings with those of Jesus Christ and you will be ashamed to complain of them. Christ did not complain, because He knew that He was suffering for you; yet you dare complain knowing, as you do, that you suffer for Christ and with Him. He suffered and He was innocent, yet He did not complain. You suffer and you are guilty, yet you complain. The sufferings that He endured were almost without number; moreover He had no one to comfort Him; your sufferings are few and easy to bear; and God sends you many graces to give you strength to bear them. Christ was taunted to come down from the cross. He could have done so had He willed it, but He preferred to remain there and die on the cross. Christ has placed you on a cross; He desires you to remain on it. You can not be assured of your salvation unless you remain there crucified with Christ; yet you make every effort to come down from that cross.

* * *

THE THOUGHT OF HEAVEN A MOTIVE OF PATIENCE

The thought of heaven ought to be a great motive of patience to one that suffers. "I beseech thee, my son, look upon heaven" (2 Mach, vii, 28) said the mother of the Machabees to one of her sons. When your sufferings are most severe, the thought of the eternal happiness which will be yours, if you bear them in the spirit of Christ, should make you rejoice to suffer. As soon as St. Paul was converted, God announced to him that He must endure great sufferings for His name. And the Apostle tells us that these sufferings were excessive. "For we would not have you ignorant, brethren, of our tribulation, which came to us in Asia, that we were pressed out of measure above our strength, so that we were weary even of life" (2 Cor. i, 8). Yet the Apostle assures us that although his sufferings were many and hard to bear, they were nothing in comparison with the recompense for which he hoped. "Superabundo gaudio in omni tribulatione nostra" (2 Cor. vii, 4). I exceedingly abound with joy in all our tribulation. In the midst of our greatest sufferings, then, should we not be filled with joy? The martyrs were so possessed by the thought of the crown they were about to receive, that they scarcely felt the torments inflicted upon them. "Vident coronas, vulnera non vident." You that are so impatient in your sufferings, meditate on the eternal happiness that awaits you.

Accustom yourself to meditate often on hell, Calvary and heaven when you feel your courage weakening in the midst of your tribulations.

"Nil sentit crux in nervo, dum animus est in coelo."—*Tertullian*. When the soul is filled with the thought of heaven, it is scarcely sensible to the sufferings of the body.

MARY AND MARTHA[2]

There were two sisters, living at Bethany near Jerusalem in the time of Our Lord, named Martha and Mary. Our Lord loved them and their brother Lazarus, and was always welcome at their home. Now at one of Our Lord's visits, Martha, being anxious to show her guest all possible hospitality, was "busy with much serving," running to and fro, arranging the banquet and apparently doing all the work, while her sister Mary was sitting quietly at Our Lord's feet, hearing His word. After a while Martha grew tired of her task, and complained to Our Lord that her sister left her all the hard work to do. So "she stood and said: Lord, hast Thou no care that my sister hath left me alone to serve? Speak to her, therefore, that she help me."

She *stood* and said these words. We can see poor Martha, out of breath, hot and tired, standing still a moment, and, somewhat ruffled in temper, thus bidding Our Lord come to the rescue. But Our Lord took Mary's part and warmly defended her, while He rebuked her elder sister. "Martha, Martha," He said—the repetition of the name suggests Our Lord's tone of voice and

---

[2]The following Reflections are excerpts from Eaton's *A Hundred Readings*

gentle look of reproach—"thou art careful, and art troubled about many things. One thing alone is necessary. Mary hath chosen the better part, which shall not be taken away from her."

This is a beautiful incident, strange at first sight, but full of instruction for all, and containing a special lesson for the sick. "Not my will, but Thine be done";—these words lie at the basis of all service of God. To love God and the task assigned to us by Him is all our duty, all our greatness, all our happiness. Our task may be that of Martha or that of Mary. Whilst you are sick, your work is certainly that of Mary, "to sit at the feet of Our Lord and hear His word," not the more active, showy work of Martha, in which perchance you gladly would busy yourself. You would wish to be up and about, to work for others, to be able to point to "something attempted, something done," day by day. All this is good, but it is not God's will for you at present: He does not seek for that fruit at your hands. Your time for this will come with the return of health and strength; meanwhile, "leaning on the bosom of Our Lord," or "sitting at His feet," you can pray and "choose the better part," for it is where God wills you to be, and at that post there is no self-seeking, no possibility of vain-glory.

"Lord, what wilt Thou have me to do?" This is the question for all, and you have your answer. Say then; "I am ready; let Him do that which is good before Him. I will not be unwise, but understanding what is the will of God." Our Lord blesses such service, and glory is given to God by every breath, by every twinge of pain. Take this lesson as sent you direct from the lips of Our Lord, and allow it to rest quietly with all its sweet encouragement in your mind and heart.

"As for me, my prayer is to Thee, O Lord, for the time of Thy good pleasure, O God. Teach me to do Thy will, for Thou art my God."

LITTLE FAULTS AND LITTLE VIRTUES

The question we have to ask ourselves is not (let us hope), "Am I going to serve God or mammon?" but "Am I ready to serve God with *all* my strength and might?" In a word, am I striving to be a saint or an *average* Christian?

What is the difference between the two? There is no question here of mortal sin, nor even much question of frequent and deliberate venial sin. The whole difference lies in the care taken over little faults and little virtues. It is the old revelation of our Divine Lord: "Well done, thou good and faithful servant," He said; and why? Because thou hast converted nations and suffered martyrdom? No. "Because thou hast been faithful over a few things, I will place thee over many." "The *little* things God *chooses* to confound the strong," to beat down the strength of pride, to annihilate the domain of self-will and self-love.

If a temptation to grave sin were to come across our path, we should instinctively shrink from it, for by its very grossness it inspires horror; and the devil knows this, and does not waste powder and shot in that direction. So, too, if a big act of virtue came before us, an opportunity to do something great and heroic, a large sacrifice to be made, there is something in its very magnitude that stirs us to face and accomplish it; we make a great effort, and it is done. Yes; but is there not at least a danger of pride and self-complacency there? And do these occasions come daily? No. To some not once in a life-time; to no one very often. Our lives are made up of trifles; the wise man is he who knows their value, the saint is he who uses them one and all, greedily and joyfully; while the average servant of God lets three parts of them slip through his fingers. Few, as St. Francis of Sales says, are the chances of making a fortune at one stroke; but day by day we may save a few pence, or at least some farthings. If we are prudent and persevere in our savings, what treasure in heaven we lay by, and that merely by avoiding little faults and by practising little virtues.

O blessed and hourly discipline of little duties, you come to us so suited to our weakness, direct from our Father's hand, as easy tasks set for the children dear to Him; you come as little victories easy to gain, and eminently calculated to encourage us, while carefully guarding us against all love of self and vain-glory, slowly but surely moulding our crown and uniting us to the Lord! Have I embraced this sweet discipline in the past? Have I not rather sought for great things and despised trifles?

And what virtues are these of which we should make so much? They are the loving and joyful acceptance of our state; the cheerful bearing with the tiresome tempers of others; the good-humored reception of little acts of selfishness or unkindness from others; gratitude when others are kind, sweetness and gentleness in speaking to all and of all, thoughtfulness and kindness to servants; care over the little acts of our spiritual life, attention at prayer. These are but examples; how ordinary they sound; how simple is their garb; but how precious in the sight of God! They are like violets that bloom in the shade of the hedgerow, but are sweet in perfume. They come to us every day, and are at hand and possible for us in time of sickness as in the day of health. And is this all that God asks of us? Yes, this is all; God will be pleased and content with that offering from our hands, and heaven is its reward.

O blessed fragments, let me gather you up, that not one be lost. Teach me, Lord, ever to value things, not for their exterior brilliancy, but for their interior motive. Let me shrink from little sins and imperfections which mar the perfection of my life and of my service of Thee. Let me aim high, striving ever after perfection by the constant practice of little acts of virtue.

* * *

Do you therefore take courage, and let not your hands be weakened; for there shall be a reward for your work.
—*2 Paral. xv, 7.*

THE LIFE OF PRAYER

Every moment of our lives belongs to God and must therefore be given to Him. Every ounce of strength, every thought, word and deed, must be directed to God's glory. He is our beginning and our end: He preserves us at each moment: we must therefore belong to Him always, serve Him at every instant, and refer all to Him. This you know well, and to accomplish it is your wish; it is only another way of saying that our lives must be lives of continual prayer.

No duty is more insisted on in Holy Scripture than that of prayer, nor is there anything more wonderful than God's love of prayer. "Pray without ceasing: be instant in prayer." "Ask and you shall receive." But you say you cannot pray much, especially when weak and in pain. Remember, then, the paths of prayer. Prayer is an offering to God, rising like clouds of incense before His throne above. And that offering goes by the path of words and thoughts, by the path of toil, and also by the path of pain and weariness. One is as good as another, provided it be pointed out by the finger of God as *the* path by which He desires *your* offering to ascend. The blind fiddler earning coppers by the roadside, the poor patient on a bed of pain—these may be leading lives of continued and beautiful prayer, as truly as the cloistered Religious who remain on bended knee for hours day by day. Believe this and act upon it; take it deeply to heart at this time; let it console and encourage you.

Humility and Patience

Qui laborat orat—"he that works also prays"—is an old and true maxim. "He that suffers with patience and resignation prays continually and well."

Probably no period of your life has been more full of merit and given more glory to God, or been so full of true prayer and done so much for sinners, as the days of your sickness. It is a penitential prayer indeed that rises from your bed to the hands of God, but remember that the lips of Our Lord, whence came His sacred words, are applied to your pain, and thence, as from some delicious fruit, He draws reparation and joy. Thus your prayer of pain is every moment bringing down graces on this poor world, by which souls are helped and saved, and all the while is registering a hundred-fold reward for you hereafter.

The Mother of Mercy

It is a joy to us all to know that we are children of Mary, made such by Our Lord at the most solemn moment in the history of the world. Our Lady is God's choicest creature, His master-piece. She holds the two-fold office of Mother of God and Mother of sinners, and she was carefully prepared for each: for the first by her sinlessness, for the second by her martyrdom, for no creature ever suffered as she did. Her life was one of poverty and daily toil; often "she had nowhere to lay her head"; and who shall say what she suffered during the hours of the Passion, when she saw her Child, "a worm and no man," scourged and defiled, bruised and derided, with the Cross bowing Him to the ground, then stripped of the robes she herself had woven for Him, and nailed to the hard wood? There she stood by Him for three hours and saw Him die, unable to do anything to ease His pain and thirst.

Why did she not then go to Heaven with Our Lord? She was left behind in this vale of tears, for she had yet a work to do for the infant Church through fifteen long years, till at length her longing was satisfied, and angels bore her home to be crowned as Queen of angels and of saints. Beautiful and "all fair" to begin with, by her martyrdom she became more lovely still, the Mother of mercy, the Mother of a pitying heart, the Mother of compassion for us her exiled children. If Mary had known no pain or desolation, she would still be splendid in our eyes, but never could she be the mother, the friend and comfort to us that she now is.

Often think of Our Lady and pray to her, especially when clouds begin to rise on the ocean that bears you home, that she, the Star of the Sea, may shine more brightly and guide and encourage you on your way. Thus does Our Lady become "our sweetness"; thus will she sweeten all that is most bitter to us, the chalice of the Passion we have to taste, and of which she drank so deeply. It is she, Our Mother, who hands to us this chalice as the healing medicine of our souls. Never are we so near to her as when near the Cross. Remember that, in our measure, we have all to suffer, and suffering must either sour or sweeten us, according as we face it. God means it to sweeten us and to teach us pity. So it worked in Mary Our Mother; so may it ever work in us, making us more full of love for God, more gentle and kind one towards another, and thus fitting us to kneel at Mary's throne when life is past.

The Apostleship of Prayer[3]

For any Catholic to be a member of the Apostleship of Prayer two conditions are requisite and sufficient; first, to get one's name registered at some Church or place where the Apostleship has been established, and to receive a ticket of admission: secondly, to make what is called the Morning Offering, that is to say, every morning in a certain definite form of oblation to offer to God all one's actions and sufferings in union with the intentions wherewith Jesus Christ offers Himself as our Victim in all the Masses said throughout the world. Nothing further is necessary to membership: but the members are further recommended to offer up every month one Communion in reparation to the Sacred Heart of Jesus for all insults and irreverences offered Him in the Holy Sacrament of the Altar. This devotion of the Morning Offering rests on the main and essential principles of Christianity:—that in "Christ we have access to the Father" (Eph. ii, 18): that "there is no salvation in any other, no other name under heaven given to man, whereby we are to be saved" (Acts iv, 12): that this salvation was wrought out by the death of Christ on the Cross, Who "made peace through the blood of His cross, blotted out the handwriting that was against us, and took it away, nailing it to the cross" (Col. i, 20: ii, 14): that this redeeming sacrifice and death of Our Saviour is continually shown forth and re-enacted in His own very Body and Blood, made present at the consecration in Holy Mass (1 Cor. xi, 24: St. Luke xxii, 19). Whenever a priest says Mass, he says it for some special intention, which he commends to God at the pause in the *Memento* for the living and for the dead. But Jesus Christ, as He is the Victim, so

---

[3] From *Ye Are Christ's* by Joseph Rickaby, S.J.

also is the Chief Priest in every Mass that is offered. He offers the Mass by the hands of his visible, mortal ministers. He then has His own intentions for every Mass that He offers, intentions sublime, wise, gracious, universal, for His Church and for mankind. But cannot He carry out His intentions without my co-operation? "Who resisteth his will" (Rom. ix, 19)? None, whenever He wills absolutely. Thus He wills absolutely to come and judge the world some day. No need of our praying for a day of judgment: "for He that is coming, will come, and will not delay" (Heb. x, 37) beyond His destined hour. But many things Our Lord intends and wills only conditionally, if men co-operate with Him. Thus He does not intend to convert the Chinese, unless missionaries go to China. Prayers are a sort of missionaries.

Many souls will be converted if they are well prayed for, and not otherwise. But the most efficacious prayer is that which goes up in closest union with Christ Crucified, pleading in sacrifice for us.

Christ Crucified thus pleads in every Mass. In every Mass, as the Church says: "the memory of His Passion is celebrated anew." I cannot spend my day in hearing Mass, traveling from altar to altar. It is not God's purpose that I should do that. But the Morning Offering of the Apostleship of Prayer, as sanctioned by the Holy See, puts me in relation with every Mass that is said that day, and lays upon every Christian altar my work and my play, my words and thoughts, my pains and sorrows, my delights and joys, and every conscious action of my will—always excepting that which is sinful, and so unacceptable, incapable of entering into holy union with the oblation of the body and blood of my Saviour. When I lie down to rest at night, I may ask myself: "Of all that I have done today, of all my goings and comings, what shall endure to my eternal good? What have I laid up in the form of treasure for heaven?" And, provided I have spent the day in the state of grace I may answer: "All and every one of my deliberate acts of will that were right in themselves, and, very signally and specially, all that has received the consecration of my morning offering." Of my strivings after the good things of this life, some will succeed, others will fail: but alike in success and failure, practising the Apostleship of Prayer, I may take to myself the Apostle's consoling words: "Be ye steadfast and immovable, always abounding in the work of the Lord, knowing that your labor is not vain in the Lord" (1 Cor. xv, 58).

Morning Offering of the Apostleship of Prayer

O Jesus, through the Immaculate Heart of Mary, I offer Thee my prayers, works and sufferings of this day for all the intentions of Thy Sacred Heart, in union with the holy sacrifice of the Mass throughout the world, in reparation for my sins, for the intentions of all our Associates, and in particular for the general intention recommended this month.

The Five Wounds

In the Transfiguration Our Saviour appeared in His glory, "and His face did shine as the sun" (Matt. xvii, 2). But one thing was wanting to Him, the print of His Five Wounds. By those Five Wounds I shall know Him, when my soul is ushered into His presence to be judged. "They shall look upon Him whom they pierced: He showed them His hands and His side" (John xix, 37: xx, 20). Thus is Jesus, even in the splendors of His Father's glory, still "the Lamb standing as if slain" (Apoc. v, 6), still "ever living to make intercession for us" (Heb. vii, 25), not, we may presume, without some reference to the Masses continually said on earth, wherein He is Chief Priest and Victim. By these Wounds I should ask for mercy when I feel I need it, as I often ought to feel. By these Wounds too I should ask mercy for my parents and friends and for my native land.

* * *

The Five Wounds were a favorite devotion in England before the Reformation, and frequently appear in such remains as we still possess of fifteenth century art. When the North of England rose in defence of the faith of their fathers against Henry VIII in what is called the Pilgrimage of Grace, the Five Wounds were embroidered on their banners. In his devotion we see the influence of the Franciscans, with whom it is still a favorite devotion, because of the *stigmata*, or impression of the Five Wounds upon the body of their glorious Founder, a miraculous favor which the Church commemorates by a yearly feast on the seventeenth of September. All the veneration and affection that we can conceive, we should pour out upon the Sacred Flesh of our Divine Saviour. Every devotion that leads us to the Flesh of Christ is good—as the Church says, "That while we know God in visible shape, we may by Him be ravished unto love of the invisible." Such a devotion is this to the Five Wounds. Those Wounds are five sources of graces flowing down from heaven to earth, as it is written: "Ye shall draw waters in joy from the fountains of the Saviour" (Isaias xii, 4)—five strong attractions drawing human hearts to God, as again Himself says: "And I, if I be lifted up from the earth, will draw all things to Myself" (John xii, 32). There is one excellent practice for me to take up. When preparing for confession, after I have examined my conscience, I frequently feel at a loss how to obtain contrition. Let me address myself to the Five Wounds of my Saviour and seek contrition there, and I shall infallibly find it.

—*Ibid.*

The Apostleship of Prayer the Perpetuation of the Work of the Incarnation[4]

Our Lord said one day to the Jews these remarkable words: "I came down from Heaven to do the will of Him that sent Me. Now this is the will of the Father Who sent Me; that of all that He hath given Me, I should lose nothing, . . . that every one who seeth the Son, and believeth in Him, may have life everlasting" (John vi, 38, 40). In these words, Our Lord distinctly makes known the purpose of His Incarnation. He came down from Heaven, He says, to do His Father's will, and then He goes on to state in what that all-holy will consists. He willed that of all that He had given to His Only Son for His heritage—all that vast humanity, all the nations and peoples and tribes of the earth, He should lose nothing; and further, that every one who sees the Son—the image of the Father—and believes in Him, may be saved. To bring this about, the Son and Our Lord came upon earth, toiled, suffered, and died.

But His passible life being ended, Jesus, our Head, having ascended into heaven, willed to leave on earth members who should perpetuate His work until the end of time, and by the same means that He had Himself employed when dwelling among us. We know how He performed His work, how He accomplished His Father's will. The greater part of His thirty-three years was spent in prayer. From the first moment of His incarnation He prayed. During His Infancy and Childhood when, having

---

[4] From The Voice of the Sacred Heart.

submitted Himself to the ordinary conditions of that early stage of life, He could perform no external work, He prayed. The eighteen years of His Hidden Life at Nazareth, dating from the time when He was found in the Temple conversing with the Doctors, were passed in the hidden apostolate of prayer, and it was by this way only that, at that period of His life, He advanced His "Father's business" which, while yet a child in years, He had declared was to Him an imperative pre-occupation. "I must be about My Father's business" (Luke ii, 49).

When He passed to His Public Life, we find Him again retiring into the mountains and spending His nights in secret converse with His Father after His days of toil, and at length when all was finished, and the hour of His supreme Sacrifice had arrived, He still prayed upon His Cross. . . . Now, when we speak of union with the Heart of Jesus, we mean union with that Heart in Its Prayer, in Its Toils, in Its Sacrifice for the glory of Him Whom Our Lord specially delighted to make known to us as our Common Father, *"My Father and your Father"* (John xx, 17).

This union of our hearts with the Heart of Jesus is peculiarly precious to Him, not only because it is a testimony of our love for Himself, personally, but likewise because it glorifies the Father by carrying on, as it were, the great work of the Incarnation, the end of which is the accomplishment of His Father's will.

"This is the will of My Father, that of all He hath given Me, I should lose nothing." . . . Assuredly if we reflected a little upon the honor and the privilege that Our Lord has conferred upon us in associating us to so noble a work, we should hardly waste our thoughts and time and energies, as it is to be feared too many among us do, upon the trifles that surround us—the empty enjoyments of this passing world, the petty miseries to which, as children of Adam, we are heirs. I say not that we should be insensible to these things, but we should not, if we were penetrated with the thought of that great mission to which each one of us, in his measure, is called, suffer our hearts and minds to be deterred by them from their legitimate preoccupation with the interests of God's glory. We should rather be induced to make of all that came in our way, a matter of self-sacrifice in union with the Sacrifice of Our Lord, for the intention for which He became Incarnate, toiled, and died.

As friends of the Sacred Heart, and Associates of Its Holy League of Prayer, this should be our one great aim and dominant solicitude: that of all that His Father has given Him for His inheritance, our Lord should lose nothing—not one of the souls, if that might be, for whom He shed His Blood; that none of His priests should ever fall from the sublime perfection of their state, nor any of those consecrated to Him in whatever way it may be, degenerate from their vocation; that the nations already possessing the true faith may never lose it, and that those as yet sitting in the darkness of heathendom may be evangelized, so that no tribe or people or nation may be excluded from the royal inheritance of the Son of God, but that all may be brought to the knowledge and love of His holy Name.

The Apostleship of the Sacred Heart is a perpetuation of the work of the Incarnation, and being so, to share in that apostleship one of the noblest aspirations, the most solid happiness, and the most sanctifying privilege that we can possess here below.

Sacred Heart of Jesus, Thy Kingdom come!

In Sickness, Suffering and Sorrow

No season is so meritorious, and therefore so fitted to enable us to make reparation to the Sacred Heart and to assist souls, as is that of sickness. Nothing, also, enables us to bear pain and all the other miseries resulting from sickness and malady, with patience and cheerfulness, so much as the thought of the interests of Jesus Christ—the needs of souls—the demand everywhere existing for prayer and voluntary suffering.

The acceptation of pain, and generous offering thereof in an apostolic spirit, will be more pleasing to the Sacred Heart, and more efficacious in promoting Its interests, than long and very devout prayers and other good works when in the enjoyment of health and strength. The holy Curé d'Ars said to a sick person: "You do more good than if you were in health; you save more souls than Père Lacordaire. You will see at the hour of death that you have saved more souls by this sickness than those who act."

Let us, then, in the long hours of weariness and pain that may be our lot, acquire the habit of making short but loving offerings of our sufferings to God, in union with those made by Our Lord during His mortal life and with His incessant immolation on the altar. The habit will become more easy to us in proportion to our fidelity and perseverance in it, until at length it will be to us a treasure of merit for ourselves, and of help to innumerable souls. A blessed Apostolate indeed is that of suffering, in whatever form it may be—sanctified, consecrated, and divinized by Jesus Christ Himself, and faithfully exercised by His Blessed Mother and all those who have followed in her footsteps.

* * *

O my God! I offer Thee this pain I am enduring, in union with those bitter torments which Thy beloved Son suffered in His Passion, and for the same intentions.

* * *

Sorrow, in whatever form it come to us, is destined by our Heavenly Father to effect a blessed and sanctifying work in our souls. But too often, alas, it is frustrated of its purpose, and instead of expanding our hearts and rendering them more meek and humble towards God and more widely and deeply compassionate towards others, unhappily it narrows our sympathies, concentrates our thoughts upon self, and engenders within us a certain apathy, if not inconsiderateness for others' sufferings. All this would be averted if we were imbued with the sentiments of the Heart of Jesus. Sorrow would then do its blessed and appointed work in our souls, and would become in us a cause of sanctification to many. That it may be thus, let us generously resolve to render the sorrows our Heavenly Father sends us, efficacious for the interests of the Sacred Heart by consecrating them to the ends of Its Apostleship.

* * *

Hail, sorrow, gift of the Sacred Heart; purify and sanctify our souls now and at the hour of our death. Amen.

* * *

O Sacred Heart! console, I beseech Thee, all those who are like me in sorrow, and teach us to sanctify our griefs for Thy greater glory.

In Temptation and Humiliation

There are no conditions and circumstances however humbling, no states of soul however painful and mortifying, which, through the goodness of God, may not be rendered subservient to the work of our Apostolate of love. If this be true, as undoubtedly it is, what an abundant source of consolation is opened to us in our temptations and other humiliations, from the knowledge that we may convert them into supplications and meritorious works for those of our brethren who are tried like ourselves. Let us cultivate an apostolic spirit in the very midst of those trials which are of a nature to discourage and depress us most.

There are humiliations which are painful indeed to our human spirit, to our natural pride and human respect, which are in reality, before God, no humiliation, but which are permitted by Him, that we may be humbled before men, and so advance in virtue. Such are misunderstandings regarding our motives or our conduct, by those in authority over us, betrayals of confidence, contempt of our abilities, of our persons, or of our affection, certain maladies or infirmities which render us troublesome or disagreeable to others, deformities and other personal disadvantages, faults, sins, and disgraces of relatives, disasters of various kinds, which seem to reflect upon our want of skill or discernment, and the like, failures of every sort, and innumerable other accidents of life which we are accustomed to regard, and which nature feels as humiliations.

When in the crucible of this kind of suffering, let us frequently make the offering of it for those under similar trials.

O God of my heart, I unite this humiliation to those Thy beloved Son supported in His mortal life, and I offer it to Thee for those souls who are enduring the same trial as myself. Give them grace to humble themselves under Thy mighty hand, that their humiliation may turn to their greater good and to Thy eternal glory.

—*Ibid.*

St. Francis Borgia, an Example of Humility and Self-Contempt[5]

Francis Borgia, Duke of Gandia, was one of the handsomest, richest and most honored nobles of Spain, when, in 1539, there was laid upon him the sad duty of escorting the remains of his sovereign, Queen Isabella, to the royal burying-place at Granada. The coffin had to be opened for him that he might verify the body before it was placed in the tomb, and so foul a sight met his eyes that he vowed never again to serve a sovereign who could suffer so base a change. It was some years before he could follow the call of his Lord; at length he entered the Society of Jesus to cut himself off from any chance of dignity or preferment. But his Order chose him to be its head. The Turks were threatening Christendom, and St. Pius V sent his nephew to gather Christian princes into a league for its defence. The holy Pope chose Francis to accompany him, and, worn out though he was, the Saint obeyed at once. The fatigues of the embassy exhausted what little life was left. St. Francis died on his return to Rome, October 10, 1572.

* * *

St. Francis Borgia learnt the worthlessness of earthly greatness at the funeral of Empress Isabella; he learnt further the dignity of Christian humility in the meditation of Our Lord's humiliation. Do the deaths of friends or the sight of the crucifix teach us aught about ourselves?

* * *

---

[5] Excerpts from Benziger Brothers' publication *Lives of the Saints* and Bowden's *Miniature Lives of the Saints*.

A Spanish nobleman said once to the Saint, "How can you bear the fatigues and hardships of your journeys, made as they are in such utter poverty?" "There is nothing to be surprised at. We do not travel so unprovided as you imagine. I always send some one on before to see to lodgings and whatever else we require." The gentleman was rather puzzled. "Sir," St. Francis added, "the knowledge of myself, and the account of my demerits, which had justly deserved the flames of hell, are my outriders and foragers."

* * *

He that hath been humbled shall be in glory; and he that shall bow down his eyes, he shall be saved.

—*Job xxii, 29.*

St. Peter Damian

By his wisdom and sanctity, St. Peter rose to be Superior of his Order. He was employed on the most delicate and difficult missions, amongst others, the reform of ecclesiastical communities, which was effected by his zeal. Seven popes in succession made him their constant adviser, and he was at last created Cardinal Bishop of Ostia.

* * *

St. Peter (born in 988), thought the greatest luminary of his age, and versed in all knowledge, profane and divine, regarded himself as the least of God's servants. Nothing less than the threat of excommunication on the part of Stephen IX induced him to accept the dignity of cardinal. And when, in deference to his urgent entreaties, he was allowed to resign his dignity and retire again to his hermitage, his whole anxiety was to be hidden among his brethren. He loved to make the wooden spoons and perform the other acts of manual labor which the Rule prescribed; and it was from such occupations that he was summoned to act as Papal Legate.

St. Paul of the Cross

The eighty-one years of this Saint's life were modeled on the Passion of Jesus Christ. In his childhood, when praying in church, a heavy bench fell on his foot, but the boy took no notice of the bleeding wound, and spoke of it as "a rose sent from God." A few years later, the vision of a scourge with "love" written on its lashes assured him that his thirst for penance would be satisfied. In the hope of dying for the faith, he enlisted in a crusade against the Turks; but a voice from the Tabernacle warned him that he was to serve Christ alone, and that he should found a congregation in His honor. At the command of his bishop he began while a layman to preach the Passion, and a series of crosses tried the reality of his vocation. All his first companions, save his brother, deserted him; the Sovereign Pointiff refused him an audience; and it was only after a delay of seventeen years that the Papal approbation was obtained, and the first house of the Passionists was opened on Monte Argentario, the spot which Our Lady had pointed out. St. Paul chose as the badge of his Order a heart with three nails, in memory of the sufferings of Jesus, but for himself he invented a more secret and durable sign. Moved by the same holy impulse as Blessed Henry Suso, St. Jane Frances, and other Saints, he branded on his side the Holy Name, and its characters were found there after death. His heart beat with a supernatural palpitation, which was especially vehement on Fridays, and the heat at times was so intense as to scorch his shirt in the region of his heart. Through fifty years of incessant bodily pain, and amidst all his trials, Paul read the love of Jesus everywhere, and would cry out to the flowers and grass, "Oh! be quiet, be quiet," as if they were reproaching him with ingratitude. He died whilst the Passion was being read to him, and so passed with Jesus from the cross to glory.

Devotion to the Passion. One sign of devotion to the Passion is a love of those souls for whom Christ died. Paul prayed and suffered specially for England, where he saw so many souls in danger of perishing by heresy and unbelief. Do we ever unite our sufferings with those of Christ for this end?

* * *

God does us great honor when He is pleased that we should tread the same road which was trodden by His only-begotten Son.
—*St. Paul of the Cross.*

* * *

With Christ I am nailed to the Cross. And I live: now not I, but Christ liveth in me.
—*Gal. ii, 19, 20.*

St. Pius V

A Dominican friar from his fifteenth year, Michael Ghisliere, as a simple Religious, as inquisitor, as bishop, and as cardinal, was famous for his intrepid defence of the Church's faith and discipline, and for the spotless purity of his own life. His first care as Pope was to reform the Roman court and capital by the strict example of his household and the severe punishment of all offenders. He next endeavored to obtain from the Catholic powers the recognition of the Tridentine decrees, two of which he urgently enforced—the residence of bishops, and the establishment of diocesan seminaries. He revised the Missal and

Breviary, and reformed the ecclesiastical music. Nor was he less active in protecting the Church without. We see him at the same time supporting the Catholic King of France against the Huguenot rebels, encouraging Mary Queen of Scots, in the bitterness of her captivity, and excommunicating her rival the usurper Elizabeth, when the best blood of England had flowed upon the scaffold, and the measure of her crimes was full. But it was at Lepanto that the Saint's power was most manifest; there, in October, 1571, by the holy league which he had formed, but still more by his prayers to the great Mother of God, the aged Pontiff crushed the Ottoman forces, and saved Christendom from the Turk. Six months later, St. Pius died, having reigned but six years.

* * *

Devotion to the Crucifix. St. Pius had always a great devotion to the crucifix, and when Pope made two meditations each day before the sacred image of Jesus suffering. There he learnt that energetic perseverance and heroic constancy which made him the saviour of the Christian world.

* * *

Thy Cross, O Lord, is the source of all blessings the cause of all graces: by it the faithful find strength in weakness, glory in shame, life in death.

—*St. Leo.*

* * *

St. Pius was accustomed to kiss the feet of his crucifix on leaving or entering his room. One day the feet moved away from his lips. Sorrow filled his heart, and he made acts of contrition, fearing that he must have committed some secret offence, but still he could not kiss the feet. It was afterwards found that they had been poisoned by an enemy.

* * *

Looking on Jesus, the Author and Finisher of faith, who having joy set before Him, endured the Cross, despising the shame, and now sitteth on the right hand of the throne of God.
—*Heb. xii, 2.*

St. Alphonsus Liguori

St. Alphonsus was born of noble parents, near Naples, in 1696. His spiritual training was intrusted to the Fathers of the Oratory in that city, and from his boyhood Alphonsus was known as a most devout Brother of the Little Oratory. At the early age of sixteen he was made doctor in law, and he threw himself into this career with ardor and success. A mistake, by which he lost an important cause, showed him the vanity of human fame, and determined him to labor only for the glory of God. He entered the priesthood, devoting himself to the most neglected souls: and to carry on this work he founded later the missionary Congregation of the Most Holy Redeemer. At the age of sixty-six he became Bishop of St. Agatha, and undertook the reform of his diocese with the zeal of a Saint. He made a vow never to lose time, and, though his life was spent in prayer and work, he composed a vast number of books, filled with such science, unction, and wisdom that he has been declared one of the Doctors of the Church. St. Alphonsus wrote his first book at the age of forty-nine, and in his eighty-third year had published about sixty volumes, when his director forbade him to write more. Very many of these books were written in the half-hours snatched from his labors as missionary, religious superior, and Bishop, or in the midst of continual bodily and mental sufferings. With his left hand he would hold a piece of marble against his aching head while his right hand wrote. Yet he counted no time wasted which was spent in charity. He did not refuse to hold a long correspondence with a simple soldier who asked his advice, or to play the harpsichord while he taught his novices to sing spiritual canticles. He lived in evil times, and met with many persecutions and disappointments. For his last seven years he was prevented by constant sickness from offering the Adorable Sacrifice; but he received Holy Communion daily, and his love for Jesus Christ and his trust in Mary's prayers sustained him to the end. He died in 1787, in his ninety-first year.

* * *

Good Use of Time. Let us do with all our heart the duty of each day, leaving the result to God, as well as the care of the future.

* * *

Consider every occasion of self-denial as a gift which God bestows on you, that you may be able to merit greater glory in another life; and remember that what can be done today cannot be performed tomorrow, for time past never returns.

—*St. Alphonsus.*

* * *

Redeeming the time, because the days are evil.
—*Eph. v, 16.*

St. Ignatius of Loyola

St. Ignatius was born at Loyola in Spain, in the year 1491. He served his king as a courtier and a soldier till his thirtieth year. At that age, being laid low by a wound, he received the call of divine grace to leave the world. He embraced poverty and humiliation, that he might become more like to Christ, and won others to join him in the service of God. Prompted by their love for Jesus Christ, Ignatius and his companions made a vow to go to the Holy Land, but war broke out, and prevented the execution of their project. Then they turned to the Vicar of Jesus Christ, and placed themselves under his obedience. This was the beginning of the Society of Jesus. Our Lord promised St. Ignatius that the precious heritage of His Passion should never fail his Society, a heritage of contradictions and persecutions. St. Ignatius went to his crown on the 31st of July, 1556.

* * *

Zeal for the Glory of God. Ask St. Ignatius to obtain for you the grace to desire ardently the greater glory of God, even though it may cost you much suffering and humiliation.

* * *

When thou shalt arrive thus far, that tribulation becomes sweet and savoury to thee for the love of Christ, then think that it is well with thee: for thou hast found a paradise on earth.

—*Imitation.*

* * *

St Ignatius was cast into prison at Salamanca on a suspicion of heresy. To a friend who expressed sympathy with him on account of his imprisonment he replied, "It is a sign that you have but little love of Christ in your heart, or you would not deem it so hard a fate to be in chains for His sake. I declare to you that all Salamanca does not contain as many fetters, manacles, and chains as I long to wear for the love of Jesus Christ."

* * *

I have glorified Thee on earth; I have finished the work which Thou gavest Me to do.
—*John xvii, 4.*

St. Columba

St. Columba, the apostle of the Picts, was born of a noble family, at Gartan, in the county of Tyrconnel, Ireland, in 521. From early childhood he gave himself to God. In all his labors—and they were many—his chief thought was heaven and how he should secure the way thither. The result was that he lay on the bare floor, with a stone for his pillow, and fasted all the year round; yet the sweetness of his countenance told of the holy soul's interior serenity. Though austere, he was not morose; and, often as he longed to die, he was untiring in good works, throughout his life. After he had been made abbot, his zeal offended King Dermot; and in 565 the Saint departed for Scotland, where he founded a hundred religious houses and converted the Picts, who in gratitude gave him the island of Iona. There St. Columba founded his celebrated monastery, the school of apostolic missionaries and martyrs, and for centuries the last resting-place of Saints and kings. Four years before his death, our Saint had a vision of angels, who told him that the day of his death had been deferred four years, in answer to the prayers of his children; whereat the Saint wept bitterly, and cried out, "Woe is me that my sojourning is prolonged!" for he desired above all things to reach his true home. How different is the conduct of most men, who dread death above everything, instead of wishing "to be dissolved, and to be with Christ"! On the day of his peaceful death, in the seventy-seventh year of his age, surrounded in choir by his spiritual children, the 9th of June, 597, he said to his disciple Diermit, "This day is called the Sabbath, that is, the day of rest, and such will it truly be to me; for it will put an end to my labors." Then, kneeling before the altar, he received the Viaticum, and sweetly slept in the Lord. His relics were carried to Down, and laid in the same shrine with the bodies of St. Patrick and St. Brigid.

Remembrance of Heaven. The thought of the world to come will always make us happy, and yet strict with ourselves in all our duties. The more perfect we become, the sooner shall we behold that for which St. Columba sighed.

* * *

It is no small matter to lose or to gain the kingdom of God.
—*Imitation.*

* * *

Eye hath not seen, nor ear heard, neither hath it entered into the heart of man, what things God hath prepared for them that love Him.
—*1 Cor. ii, 9.*

St. Francis Xavier

A young Spanish gentleman, in the dangerous days of the Reformation, was making a name for himself as a Professor of Philosophy in the University of Paris, and had seemingly no higher aim, when St. Ignatius of Loyola won him to heavenly thoughts. After a brief apostolate amongst his countrymen in Rome he was sent by St. Ignatius to the Indies, where for twelve years he was to wear himself out, bearing the Gospel to Hindostan, to Malacca, and to Japan. Thwarted by the jealousy, covetousness, and carelessness of those who should have helped and encouraged him, neither their opposition nor the difficulties of every sort which he encountered could make him slacken his labors for souls. The vast kingdom of China appealed to his charity, and he was resolved to risk his life to force an entry, when God took him to Himself, and on the 2nd of December, 1552, he died, like Moses, in sight of the land of promise.

* * *

Thirst for Souls. Some are specially called to work for souls; but there is no one who cannot help much in their salvation. Holy example, earnest intercession, the offerings of our actions in their behalf—all this needs only the spirit which animated St. Francis Xavier, the desire to make some return to God.

If God bids us rather lose our own life than give up the salvation of souls, we are determined to obey His command, with His own good assistance, and supplied by Him with strength and courage.

—*St. Francis Xavier.*

* * *

A Portuguese gentleman once sailed in the same ship with St. Francis Xavier, and was very anxious to see the famous missionary. Great was his disappointment on being shown a person standing in a group round a chess-table, chatting familiarly with the soldiers, crew, and passengers, like any ordinary priest. At the end of the voyage, however, he sent his servant to see what became of him. Francis went aside into a wood and began to pray, and the servant soon ran to call his master to see the Saint in an ecstasy lifted from the ground in his prayers.

* * *

Therefore I endure all things for the sake of the elect, that they also may obtain the salvation which is in Christ Jesus, with heavenly glory.

—2 Tim. ii, 10.

St. Peter Claver

Peter Claver was a Spanish Jesuit. In Majorca he fell in with the holy lay-brother Alphonsus Rodriguez, who, having already learned by revelation the saintly career of Peter, became his spiritual guide, foretold to him the labors he would undergo in the Indies, and the throne he would gain in heaven. Ordained priest in New Granada, Peter was sent to Cartagena, the great slave-mart of the West Indies, and there he consecrated himself by vow to the salvation of those ignorant and miserable creatures—the slaves. For more than forty years he labored in this work. He called himself "the slave of the slaves." He was their apostle, father, physician, and friend. He fed them, nursed them with the utmost tenderness in their loathsome diseases, often applying his own lips to their hideous sores. His cloak, which was the constant covering of the naked, though soiled with their filthy ulcers, sent forth a miraculous perfume. However tired he might be, when news arrived of a fresh slave-ship, St. Peter immediately revived, his eyes brightened, and he was at once on board amongst his dear slaves, bringing them comfort for body and soul. A false charge of reiterating Baptism for a while stopped his work. He submitted without a murmur till the calumny was refuted, and then God so blessed his toil that 40,000 Negroes were baptized before he went to his reward, in 1654.

* * *

Charity to Our Neighbor. When you see any one standing in need of your assistance, either for body or soul, do not ask yourself why some one else did not help him, but think to yourself that you have found a treasure.

* * *

Do thou seek nothing in the world save that which Jesus Christ Himself has sought—to sanctify souls, to work, to suffer, nay, to die for their salvation.

—St. Peter Claver.

* * *

When Easter came, St. Peter left the town to search the mountains for the Negroes who might be scattered among them. The tropical storms drenched him to the skin, but he never turned nor stopped. When he found a settlement he would never leave it till the last Negro was brought to the Sacrament of Penance. He once suddenly left the house where he was staying, and plunged without guide or road into impracticable mountain recesses. None knew whither or why he went; but when he returned pale and worn, it was discovered that he had gone to administer the last Sacraments to three old Negroes who had been abandoned by all the world and had crawled into a ruined hut to die.

Who is weak, and I am not weak? Who is scandalized, and I am not on fire?

—2 Cor. xi, 29.

St. Elizabeth of Hungary

Elizabeth was daughter of a king of Hungary, and niece of St. Hedwige. She was betrothed in infancy to Louis, Landgrave of Thuringia, and brought up in his father's court. Not content with receiving daily numbers of poor in her palace, and relieving all in distress, she built several hospitals, where she served the sick, dressing the most repulsive sores with her own hands. Once as she was carrying in the folds of her mantle some provisions for the poor, she met her husband returning from the chase. Astonished to see her bending under the weight of her burden, he opened the mantle which she kept pressed against her, and found in it nothing but beautiful red and white roses, although it was not the season for flowers. Bidding her pursue her way, he took one of the marvelous roses, and kept it all his life. On her husband's death she was cruelly driven from her palace, and forced to wander through the streets with her little children, a prey to hunger and cold; but she welcomed all her sufferings, and continued to be the mother of the poor, converting many by her holy life. She died in 1231, at the age of twenty-four.

* * *

Love of the Poor. This young and delicate princess made herself the servant and nurse of the poor. Let her example teach us to disregard the opinions of the world and to overcome our natural repugnances, in order to serve Jesus Christ in the persons of His poor.

* * *

A tender love of our neighbor is one of the greatest and most excellent gifts that the Divine Goodness bestows upon men.
—*St. Francis of Sales.*

* * *

The truly patient man minds not by whom he is tried; whether by his superior, or by an inferior; whether by a good and holy man, or by one that is perverse and unworthy.

—Imitation.

* * *

Eat thy bread with the hungry and the needy, and with thy garments cover the naked.

—Tobias iv, 17.

St. Helen

It was the pious boast of the city of Colchester, England, for many ages, that St. Helen was born within its walls; and though this honor has been disputed, it is certain that she was a British princess. She embraced Christianity late in life: but her incomparable faith and piety greatly influenced her son Constantine, the first Christian emperor, and served to kindle a holy zeal in the hearts of the Roman people. Forgetful of her high dignity, she delighted to assist at the Divine Office amid the poor; and by her alms-deeds showed herself a mother to the indigent and distressed. In her eightieth year she made a pilgrimage to Jerusalem, with the ardent desire of discovering the cross on which our blessed Redeemer suffered. After many labors, three crosses were found on Mount Calvary, together with the nails and the inscription recorded by the Evangelists. It still remained to identify the true cross of Our Lord. By the advice of the bishop, Macarius, the three were applied successively to a woman afflicted with an incurable disease, and no sooner had the third touched her than she arose, perfectly healed. The pious empress, transported with joy, built a most glorious church on Mount Calvary to receive the precious relic, sending portions of it to

Rome and Constantinople, where they were solemnly exposed to the adoration of the faithful. Shortly after, Helen herself returned to Rome, where she expired, 328.

* * *

Devotion to the Holy Cross. St. Helen thought it the glory of her life to find the cross of Christ, and to raise a temple in its honor. How many Christians in these days are ashamed to make this life-giving sign, and to confess themselves the followers of the Crucified!

* * *

O admirable power of the Cross, the ineffable glory of the Passion, in which is the judgment-seat of God, the condemnation of the world, and the virtue of the Crucified.

In the year 312 Constantine found himself attacked by Maxentius with vastly superior forces, and the very existence of his empire threatened. In this crisis he bethought him of the crucified Christian God whom his mother Helen worshipped; and kneeling down, prayed God to reveal Himself and give him the victory. Suddenly, at noonday, a cross of fire was seen by his army in the calm and cloudless sky, and beneath it the words. *In hoc signo vinces*—"Through this sign thou shalt conquer." By divine command Constantine made a standard like the cross he had seen, which was borne at the head of his troops; and under this Christian ensign they marched against the enemy, and obtained a complete victory.

* * *

He humbled Himself, becoming obedient unto death, even to the death of the Cross.

—Phil. ii, 8.

St. John of the Cross

The father of St. John was discarded by his kindred for marrying a poor orphan, and the Saint, thus born and nurtured in poverty, chose it also for his portion. Unable to learn a trade, he became the servant of the poor in the hospital of Medina, while still pursuing his sacred studies. In 1563, being then twenty-one, he humbly offered himself as a lay-brother to the Carmelite friars, who, however, knowing his talents, had him ordained priest. He would now have exchanged to the severe Carthusian Order, had not St. Teresa, with the instinct of a Saint, persuaded him to remain and help her in the reform of his own Order. Thus he became the first prior of the Barefooted Carmelites. His reform, though approved by the general, was rejected by the elder friars, who condemned the Saint as a fugitive and apostate, and cast him into prison, whence he only escaped, after nine months' suffering, at the risk of his life. Twice again, before his death, he was shamefully persecuted by his brethren, and publicly disgraced. But his complete abandonment by creatures only deepened his interior peace and devout longing for heaven.

* * *

Perfect Detachment. "Live in the world," said St. John, "as if God and your soul only were in it; so shall your heart be never made captive by any earthly thing."

* * *

The Saint hearing the voice of Christ say, "John, what reward shall I give thee for all thy labors?" replied, "Lord, to suffer and be despised for Thy sake."

* * *

When St. John was in his last illness, he was given the choice of one of two convents where he should repair for treatment. The one at Baeza was convenient in every way, and the prior was his intimate friend. The other, at Ubeda, was distant and poor; and the prior, F. Diego, was his bitter enemy. He chose the latter. The fatigue of the journey increased the wounds in his leg, which caused him intense pain; yet the prior locked him up for three months in a little cell, and forbade him all relief. Here he lingered, till released by the Provincial a few days before his death, when the prior was himself converted by his invincible patience. Then the Saint prepared with joy to die, and crucifix in hand, with the words, "Glory be to God!" he breathed forth his soul, A.D. 1591, being then forty-nine years old. St. Teresa says, "He was one of the purest souls in the Church of God."

* * *

I know thy tribulation and thy poverty; but thou art rich.
—*Apoc. ii, 9.*

St. Andrew Avellino

After a holy youth, Lancelot Avellina was ordained priest at Naples. At the age of thirty-six he entered the Theatine Order, and took the name of Andrew, to show his love for the cross. For fifty years he was afflicted with a most painful rupture; yet he would never use a carriage. Once when he was carrying the Viaticum, and a storm had extinguished the lamps, a heavenly light encircled him, guided his steps, and sheltered him from the rain. But as a rule, his sufferings were unrelieved by God or man. In his last illness he lay on hard boards, praying for a good death, and assaulted by demons tempting him to despair. At last, on November 10, 1608, he died in peace.

Preparation for Death. St. Andrew, who suffered so terrible an agony, is the special patron against sudden death. Ask him to be with you in your last hour, and to bring Jesus and Mary to your aid.

* * *

He who hourly awaits death, even if he die suddenly, will not fail to die well.

—*St. Alphonsus Liguori.*

* * *

On the last day of his life St. Andrew rose, in spite of his sufferings, to say Mass. He was in his eighty-ninth year, and so weak that he could scarcely reach the altar; yet none liked to thwart the purpose of the holy old man. He began the "Judica," and fell forward in a fit of apoplexy. Laid on a straw mattress he foamed at the mouth, and his whole frame was convulsed in agony, while the fiend in visible form advanced to seize his soul. Then, as his brethren prayed and wept, the voice of Mary was heard, bidding the Saint's guardian angel send the tempter back to hell. The fiend slunk back in despair. A calm and holy smile settled on the features of the dying Saint as, with a grateful salutation to the image of Mary, he breathed forth his soul to God.

* * *

Before thy death work justice, for in hell there is no finding food.

—*Ecclus. xiv, 17.*

St. Bruno

Bruno was born at Cologne, about 1030, of an illustrious family. He was endowed with rare natural gifts, which he cultivated with care at Paris. He became canon of Cologne, and then of Rheims, where he had the direction of theological studies. On the death of the bishop the see fell for a time into evil hands, and Bruno retired with a few friends into the country. There he resolved to forsake the world, and to live a life of retirement and penance. With six companions he applied to Hugh, Bishop of Grenoble, who led them into a wild solitude called the Chartreuse. There they lived in poverty, self-denial, and silence, each apart in his own cell, meeting only for the worship of God, and employing themselves in copying books. From the name of the spot the Order of St. Bruno was called the Carthusian. Six years later, Urban II called Bruno to Rome, that he might avail himself of his guidance. Bruno tried to live there as he had lived in the desert; but the echoes of the great city disturbed his solitude, and, after refusing high dignities, he wrung from the Pope permission to resume his monastic life in Calabria. There he lived, in humility and mortification and great peace, till his blessed death in 1101.

* * *

The Remembrance of Eternity. "O everlasting kingdom," said St. Augustine; "kingdom of endless ages, whereon rests the untroubled light and the peace of God which passeth all understanding, where the souls of the Saints are in rest, and everlasting joy is on their heads, and sorrow and sighing have fled away! When shall I come and appear before God?"

* * *

Eternity is stamped upon the minds of Saints by gazing on the eternity of God.

—*St. Gregory.*

* * *

St. Hugh of Grenoble spent so much time at the Chartreuse that St. Bruno, who was his director, recommended him to return to his diocese. The Count of Nevers made a long stay with them to learn how to serve God with more fervor; and on his return home he was so affected by the remembrance of their extreme poverty, that he sent them many costly gifts and much plate. The Saint sent back the gifts, saying that they were simply useless to them. The Count then sent them a quantity of parchments and leather, to be used in copying books, by which they gained their subsistence.

* * *

I thought upon the days of old; and I had in my mind the eternal years.

—*Ps. ixxvi, 6.*

Remember

Remember these words of Holy Writ: *"Be you also ready, because at what hour you know not the Son of man will come"* (Matt. xxiv, 44).

Very quickly must thou be gone from hence, see then how matters stand with thee; a man is here today and tomorrow he is vanished (1 Mach, ii, 63).

And when he is taken away from the sight he is quickly also out of mind.

Oh, the dullness and hardness of man's heart, which only thinks of what is present, and looks not forward to things to come.

Thou oughtst in every action and thought so to order thyself as if thou wert immediately to die.

If thou hadst a good conscience thou wouldst not much fear death.

It were better for thee to fly sin than to be afraid of death (Dan. xiii, 23).

If thou art not prepared today how shalt thou be tomorrow?

Tomorrow is an uncertain day; and how dost thou know that thou shalt be alive tomorrow? (James iv, 14).

What benefit is it to live long when we advance so little?

Ah! long life does not always make us better, but often adds to our guilt.

Would to God we had behaved ourselves well in this world even for one day!

Many count the years of their conversion; but oftentimes the fruit of amendment is but small.

If it be frightful to die, perhaps it will be more dangerous to live longer.

Blessed is he that has always the hour of death before his eyes and every day disposes himself to die (Ecclus. vii, 40).

If thou hast at any time seen a man die think that thou must also pass the same way.

In the morning imagine that thou shalt not live till night; and when evening comes presume not to promise thyself the next morning.

Be therefore always prepared, and live in such a manner that death may never find thee unprovided.

Many die suddenly and when they little think of it.

"When that last hour shall come, thou wilt begin to have quite other thoughts of thy whole past life; and thou wilt be exceedingly grieved that thou hast been so negligent and remiss" (Wis. v, 6).

How happy and prudent is he who strives to be such now in this life as he desires to be found at his death.

For it will give a man a great confidence of dying happily if he has a perfect contempt of the world, a fervent desire of advancing in virtue, a love for discipline, the spirit of penance, a ready obedience, self-denial, and patience in bearing all adversities for the love of Christ.

Thou mayst do many good things whilst thou art well, but when thou art sick I know not what thou wilt be able to do.

Few are improved by sickness.

Trust not in thy friends and relations, nor put off the welfare of thy soul to hereafter; for men will sooner forget thee than thou imaginest.

"It is better now to provide in time, and send some good before thee, than to trust to the help of others after thy death" (Matt. vi, 20).

If thou art not now careful for thyself who will be careful for thee hereafter?

The present time is very precious, "now is an acceptable time: now is the day of salvation" (2 Cor. vi, 2).

"Chastise thy body now by penance that thou mayst then have an assured confidence" (1 Cor. ix, 27).

"Ah fool! why dost thou think to live long when thou art not sure of one day?" (Luke xii, 20).

How many thinking to live long have been deceived and unexpectedly snatched away.

How often hast thou heard related that such a man was slain by the sword; another drowned; another falling from on high broke his neck; this man died at the table; that other came to his end when he was at play.

"Some have perished by fire; some by the sword; some by pestilence; some by robbers; and thus death is the end of all, and man's life passeth suddenly like a shadow" (Eccles. vii, 1).

Who will remember thee when thou art dead and who will pray for thee?

Do now, beloved, do now all thou canst, because thou knowest not when thou shalt die; nor dost thou know what shall befall thee after death.

"There are just men and wise men, and their works are in the hand of God—and yet man knoweth not whether he be worthy of love or hatred." "Whilst thou hast time, heap to thyself riches that will never die" (Matt. vi, 20).

Make now to thyself friends by honoring the saints of God and by imitating their actions, "that when thou shalt fail in this life they may receive thee into everlasting dwellings" (Luke xvi, 9).

"Keep thyself as a pilgrim, and a stranger upon earth to whom the affairs of this world do not belong" (1 Peter ii, 11).

Keep thy heart free and raised upwards to God, because thou hast not here a lasting abode.

"Send thither thy daily prayers, with sighs and tears, that after death thy spirit may be worthy to pass happily to Our Lord" (Thomas à Kempis).

Prayer

O God, grant that I may be ever mindful of the eternal years, and that, as a pilgrim destined for the Heavenly Jerusalem, I may adhere unflinchingly to the royal road of the cross, pushing onward and upward bravely and cheerfully, keeping my eyes uplifted to the everlasting hills, trusting in Thee, and looking for help from Thee, O holy God, O good God, O strong God.

The Eternal Years

How shalt thou bear the Cross that now
  So dread a weight appears?
Keep quietly to God, and think
  Upon the Eternal Years.

Austerity is little help,
  Although it somewhat cheers;
Thine oil of gladness is the thought
  Of the Eternal Years.

Set hours and written rule are good,
  Long prayer can lay our fears:
But it is better calm for thee
  To count the Eternal Years.

Rites are as balm unto the eyes,
  God's work unto the ears:
But He will have thee rather brood
  Upon the Eternal Years.

Full many things are good for souls

In proper times and spheres;
Thy present good is in the thought
  Of the Eternal Years.

Bear gently, suffer like a child,
  Nor be ashamed of tears;
Kiss the sweet Cross, and in thy heart
  Sing of the Eternal Years.

Thy Cross is quite enough for thee.
  Though little it appears;
For there is hid in it the weight
  Of the Eternal Years.

And knowest thou not how bitterness
  An ailing spirit cheers?
Thy medicine is the strengthening thought
  Of the Eternal Years.

One Cross can sanctify a soul;
  Late saints and ancient seers
Were what they were, because they mused
  Upon the Eternal Years.

Pass not from flower to pretty flower;
  Time flies, and judgment nears;
Go! make thy honey from the thought
  Of the Eternal Years.

Death will have rainbows round it, seen
  Through calm contrition's tears,

If tranquil hope but trims her lamp
　At the Eternal Years.

A single practice long sustained
　A soul to God endears:
This must be Thine—to weigh the thought
　Of the Eternal Years.

He practises all Virtue well
　Who his own Cross reveres,
And lives in the familiar thought
　Of the Eternal Years.

—Father Faber.

Home, Sweet Home

The thought of death is a strong thought, but not at all a depressing one; it makes life real, not gloomy; it gives meaning and tone to all we do, and should never be long banished from our minds. Our Blessed Lord, "who has made all things new," has quite changed the aspect of death. Before His time it was regarded with sheer dread and horror as a punishment and nothing more. It remains a punishment, but is now seen to be for "faithful servants" a passage to a mansion in our Father's house, a going home, a commendation of an immortal soul most dear to God and redeemed by the Precious Blood into the hands of its Maker, where it shall find eternal rest. "Father, into Thy hands I commend my spirit." Death is this or ought so to be: death is gain, if "to live has been Christ," for "the sting of death is sin." It is in the new aspect of death that the finishing touch is put to our Lord's great work for us. Not life only, but death too is lit up by

His teaching. The two go together, and expand into eternity like a river flowing into the sea.

Meanwhile we are pilgrims on the way, hand in hand with one another, hand in hand with our Lord, guided by clear rules of conduct, with timely warnings as to dangers, with an abundance of food, in the company of Our Lady and many angels and saints, daily approaching nearer to the end, marching to certain victory if we are faithful to the end. We must always be ready, yet never in a hurry: "be you ready, for you know not the day nor the hour." Let God decide for us: can we not trust Him? Our part is to work on contentedly, always saying: "What shall I wish to have done when I come to die?" This will help us in pain, in temptation, and in receiving the Sacraments. "Think on thy last end and thou shalt never sin." "Short years," says holy Job, "pass away, and I am walking in a path by which I shall not return." "O Lord, make me know my end, and what is the number of my days, that I may know what is wanting to me." Under the eye of Our Lord, knowing that He has "a care for us," let us daily "provide for our last end," being moulded according to what He wishes; and at the moment that is best for us, He will open the narrow gate and welcome us home.

—Eaton: A Hundred Readings.

AVE MARIA

Ave Maria! the night shades are falling,
   Softly our voices arise unto thee
Earth's lonely exiles for succor are calling,
   Sinless and beautiful, Star of the Sea!
    Mater Amabilis, ora pro nobis!

Ave Maria! thy children are kneeling.
   Words of endearment are murmured to thee;
Softly thy spirit upon us is stealing,
   Sinless and beautiful, Star of the Sea.
    Mater Amabilis, ora pro nobis!

Ave Maria! thou portal of Heaven,
   Harbor of refuge, to thee do we flee;
Lost in the darkness, by stormy winds driven,
   Shine on our pathway, fair Star of the Sea!

Mater Amabilis, ora pro nobis!
   Pray for thy children who call upon thee;
Ave Sanctissima! Ave purissima!
   Sinless and beautiful, Star of the Sea.

JESU, DEUS MEUS, SUPER OMNIA AMO TE!

Printed in Great Britain
by Amazon